THE RADIO DOCUMENTARY HANDBOOK

Creating, producing, and selling for broadcast

Jurgen Hesse

SELF-COUNSEL SERIES

International Self-Counsel Press Ltd.
Vancouver   Toronto

Self-Counsel Press Ltd.
Seattle

Printed in Canada

Printed in Canada   **713488**

First edition: February, 1987

Canadian Cataloguing in Publication Data

Hesse, Jurgen.
    The radio documentary handbook

    (Self-counsel series)
    ISBN 0-88908-653-2

    1. Documentary radio programs.   I. Title.   II. Series.
PN1991.8.D6H48 1987   791.4'45   C86-091523-9

Cover design by Sara Woodwark
Illustrations by Dave Alavoine

SELF-COUNSEL SERIES

International Self-Counsel Press Ltd.
Editorial Office
1481 Charlotte Road
North Vancouver
British Columbia V7J 1H1
Canada

Self-Counsel Press Inc.
1303 N. Northgate Way
Seattle
Washington, U.S.A. 98133
(a subsidiary of International Self-Counsel Press Ltd.)

CONTENTS

LIST OF SAMPLES

LIST OF ILLUSTRATIONS

ACKNOWLEDGMENTS

This book is more than one man's summary of experience as a radio broadcaster, documentarist and writer. Rather, it represents the distillation of many years of dedicated, high caliber work by several people who helped me become a competent professional in the field of radio.

Leading this group of radio producers and sound engineers is Don Mowatt, with whom I have worked since 1972, developing a distinctive radio documentary and feature style. Our creative collaboration has lead to some successful teamwork, even though I am a notorious loner. We inspired each other, but it remains for me to thank this CBC producer — a radio artist.

Other thanks go to James Reid, who, in my opinion, is one of the great sound engineers. I have worked with Mr. Reid for many years, and the results are evident to all listeners to CBC Radio, where productions emerging from the Mowatt-Reid-Hesse collaboration have been broadcast.

There are many others who have contributed through the years since 1961 when I began my radio career in Canada.

Novelists, filmmakers and documentarists all know the feeling when a project has been finished, the result works well, and the author can sit back, twiddle his or her thumbs and think: "It's done. All the work came together. Timing's good. Fine. Now on to the next one."

INTRODUCTION

Radio is a convenient medium. You can listen to it while in the car and on the go, or while doing something else, such as ironing a shirt. Because you devote only one sense to radio — hearing — the other four senses can keep on working at something else while you listen.

Radio is also an intimate medium. It can keep you company when you are alone — simply sit back, close your eyes, and concentrate on nothing but sound.

These are only two reasons why listeners enjoy radio. There are other reasons why some journalists prefer to work in this medium.

Perhaps it is because radio is an affordable medium. Unlike television with its prohibitive production costs, you can create some of the most avant-garde, stimulating and challenging radio productions for minimum cost.

Or perhaps it is because radio is a creative medium. Radio must compete with other media for our attention and has, as a result, become increasingly imaginative. Relative to broadcast technology when radio first became popular earlier in this century, today's radio journalists use an arsenal of tools to put words, music and sound on air. Yet radio technology remains simple and direct.

Radio is unbeaten in speed and immediacy. You can move from event to tape to broadcast in a matter of seconds.

As a result, today the radio industry attracts some of the most capable actors, writers, technicians and sound engineers available.

This book can help you enter the field of radio with radio documentaries. Through reading this book you will learn how to develop an idea, how to write a proposal to sell that idea, how to research facts and background information, how to interview people using a microphone, how to handle tape recorders and edit tape, and how to assemble all these components into a montage of creative sound for broadcast. In short, this book will give you detailed guidelines to help you fashion an idea into a radio program.

Use the information contained in this handbook and you will acquire all the skills that make a radio journalist. Provided you have ideas, self-discipline, perseverance, and organization you can look to an exciting future as a broadcast journalist.

1

THE IDEA'S THE THING

Before you can produce a radio documentary through all its many phases, you must have a compelling idea. That idea will be the current that makes a light bulb glow; it will literally electrify you into action.

a. FROM CONCEPT TO PRODUCT

On October 30, 1938, Orson Welles demonstrated the awesome power of a good idea expressed on radio. In his radio adaptation of H. G. Wells's novel, *War of the Worlds*, Orson Welles carefully constructed an atmosphere of stark terror when he broadcast a fictional news report of Wells's invasion of the world by Martians. Orson Welles proved his concept that radio drama, disguised as fact, could terrorize people into believing almost anything. From that concept, Welles produced a radio broadcast that has become a classic.

Orson Welles's radio adaptation of *War of the Worlds* is a good example of an idea taken from concept through development to fruition. You too can conceive an idea and develop it into a radio broadcast. But that radio broadcast must be a story well told, impeccably researched, based on fact, assembled with skill, and presented with panache.

b. AN IDEA IS BORN

But where do ideas come from? Ideas are based on knowledge and experience. Because journalists depend on ideas for their livelihood they first depend on a good education in as wide a field as possible. Then anything can inspire an idea — newspapers, weeklies, magazines, throwaways, trade journals, government reports, advertisements, junk mail, even the labels on food cans. Any words and images your eyes come across can spark an idea.

Despite the new technologies of the computer, the micro-chip, and the ever-increasing potency of software programs with their mega- and giga-byte storage capacity, the human mind is still the best storage facility. Your spark of inspiration conceives an idea, then it is processed in your own databank, called memory. The more you are able to employ your memory to select relevant and irrelevant facts, the more your home-grown computer is able to exploit a databank of knowledge and experience, and to shuffle the facts around until they form a new usable pattern. The more fully we can activate our built-in software program called creative thinking, the more often we come up with an idea that works.

Here is an example: You want to submit a proposal for a radio broadcast. You sit at your desk, waiting for an idea to formulate. You need that idea. You look out the window. There you see a billboard advertising product XYZ. The image and the words of the ad trigger a memory, and an idea is born. You feed your fledgling idea with associative sparks of inspiration and nurture it into being.

This process is called brainstorming. Most people think you need a committee to engage in a brainstorming session. Wrong. You can brainstorm all by yourself. If need be, doodle; talk to yourself; sing; get up and wave your arms around; exercise; make a sandwich — and Bang!, suddenly your idea becomes a proposal you can submit to a radio producer. You are on your way to a contract, work, and money in the bank.

c. DOING YOUR HOMEWORK

Before you can explore the wonderful world of ideas, you must do some footslogging work. You must first read about and listen to what is going on around you.

Hundreds of young men and women appear at the door of radio stations every year. Many approach the reception area and ask if there is any work. Some venture beyond the receptionist and see the personnel officer. The more determined ones advance to the producers' offices, interrupting producers at work, asking them whether there are any jobs.

Experienced radio producers know the quickest way to get rid of job applicants is to ask, "Did you listen to my program last week?" Nine times out of ten the applicants admit they did not. Why not? You would think it obvious to do this kind of basic research before going job hunting. Yet not enough hopeful radio journalists-to-be listen to the radio.

If you want to be a radio broadcaster, tune in, find out what the current trend is in broadcast ideas.

- Go to meetings of professional associations for the electronic media; for example, in the U.S., attend meetings of the Writers Guild of America East and West, and in Canada, those of the Alliance of Canadian Cinema, Television and Radio Artists (ACTRA). Go as a guest first, get to know the members, make friends, discuss your aspirations and ask for advice. Most broadcasters, even fairly busy ones, will take time to help if you ask them.

- Attend workshops. School boards, colleges and universities offer excellent adult learning classes for aspiring writers and broadcasters. By attending them you can learn the basics from experienced professionals who enjoy teaching.

- Hang out with pros. You may have friends or relatives who work in radio. Ask to accompany them on assignments; look over their shoulders as they prepare their material, edit tape, choose music, whatever. If you have no such connections, go to your local radio station, ask to speak with the manager, explain that you're keen to learn, and watch. Most will be glad to help you out by introducing you to the technician, the deejay, the story editor, *and* the producer.

- Offer to work as a volunteer at a campus, co-operative, or community radio station. You will be exposed to daily procedures, learn quickly, and start making connections. Volunteers are much appreciated because they don't cost the station money and are usually keen to develop a basis for future employment.

- Find a mentor. Latch on to an experienced broadcaster, not by ingratiating yourself, but by asserting your hopes for a similar career. Such limited, tasteful flattery will often be rewarded. Many young broadcast journalists have benefited from such mature associations.

Most important, though, listen to radio for an entire week, make notes, compare, weigh, and juggle the results. But listen. Without this basic research you have little chance of coming up with an idea that can be sold, produced, and broadcast.

d. FINDING AN ANGLE

An idea is only as good as the angle that makes it work. An angle is like a secret ingredient; it is the yeast that makes dough rise. There are myriad ideas, most of which have been tried before in broadcasting. But a specific angle elevates an idea from mediocrity to an exciting prospect. And the best idea peddlers are those who offer something new to those in the market for ideas.

Here is an example to demonstrate how an angle can work: A man threatened to jump from a downtown office tower. The city editor sent a reporter to cover the event for his newspaper. So did a lot of other city editors because there were about 12 media people at the site. After three hours of agony, the man was persuaded to climb down.

Throughout the event, the reporter took notes, jotting down the times each new event happened: the arrival of the fire fighters, the man's wife and son, a psychiatrist, the family priest, the man's brother; the passing car; and the drunk who shouted, "Hey buddy, why doncha jump?"

The angle the reporter used was the drama of the waiting game: would he or would he not jump? To come up with this angle, the reporter remembered a story he had read in the *New Yorker*, which described a similar media event for some 10 pages. On a routine assignment he had used his memory, found an idea, and discovered a new angle. He wrote the story, which his city editor truly appreciated. Meanwhile, the other media people missed the angle. It happens all the time.

e. DEVELOPING AN IDEA

This book represents the product of my having and pursuing an idea. When I was teaching a university course on how to make radio documentaries, I thought it would be useful for my students to have a few printed pages in which the basics were explained, but there was nothing in print.

That was when I had the idea to write my own short guideline. Soon the original idea mushroomed and the few pages grew into another idea to write a book. One idea gained momentum.

The same applies when you want to become a radio journalist. It all begins with an idea; that idea often leads to another, and the rest is applied routine.

Let's look at the stages through which an idea must pass before it becomes a radio program. First, you must kick a basic idea around, look at it from all sides, and discuss it with other people you trust if you're not quite sure whether your idea will work. If you cannot depend on your memory to tell you whether someone else has had the same idea, spend some time in the public library's periodical and daily newspaper file. Look for obvious cross-references, similar stories, and related events. (See chapter 5, Doing the Research.)

Instinct, another aspect of developing an idea, comes into play. For instance, suppose you are walking downtown and you notice a large number of street vendors, musicians, panhandlers, and odd characters who have a particular religious or political message. "Bingo!" you think. "I could make a radio documentary about all these colorful personalities."

Fine. Except that the producer in the market for radio programs will likely look at you and say, "You are the twenty-seventh person who has suggested this idea to me. Come back when you think up something original." If you try to sell an idea that is new to you but suffers from terminal repetition, it shows bad planning and tends to lower your future credibility.

You must progress from the commonplace to the unique, from a well-used idea to an original concept. For an idea to have saleable merit, it must have that certain oomph, that little twist that lifts it out of the ordinary and makes it into something novel and irresistible.

Suppose you notice during your downtown stroll that one of the panhandlers doesn't look genuine. Something about him doesn't sit well with you; you decide to go home and mull it over. Perhaps in the middle of the night you sit bolt upright because you realize the panhandler you saw used to be a prominent, well-connected businessperson in town. You may have a human interest story on your hands.

Or suppose, instead of the prominent businessperson, you realize the panhandler is a local politician who has decided to live on welfare for a month to see how hard it is, and he hasn't told the media about his experiment. Then you have a scoop.

These two stories developed out of instinct. A journalist without instinct is like a rose without color and scent. Instinct is an indefinable, sixth sense. It twigs when some of the data your other senses feed back don't quite compute. You may not recognize what's wrong right away, but you will not let it go; you will worry about it, think about it, and sit on it until something clicks into place.

Once an idea grabs you and won't let go, you will discover that an idea is mightier than creature comforts. You will find yourself walking around in a daze, making hasty notes, mumbling to yourself, and generally acting strange. If your idea germinates to the stage where it takes off and assumes a life of its own, then you are at the start of an exciting project. Give in to instinct; the resulting idea may become a project.

f. FROM IDEA TO SCOOP

The idea, thin as it was at the outset, now embroidered with unerring instinct, has suddenly become either a solid human interest story or a scoop. Both stories mean you have an original idea worth offering for sale.

But you must first take one more important step. You must determine whether the idea will work. You might be tempted to ask, "How can it not work?" Let's look at the two potential panhandler stories more closely:

Panhandler No. 1 The businessperson, scion of a powerful clan in your city, is an alcoholic and has taken to the streets in search of money for booze. His family has abandoned him. You sense a big story.

You could start recording his incoherent mumblings, ignoring the uneasy stirrings of your conscience telling you to be decent and to remember that this person is a human being with a common social problem. If you make the plight of this person public, you will at best put a few dollars in your pocket and at worst turn the whole city against you. You will lose your reputation, and your poor judgment will stick with you for years to come, in the most unexpected places.

Keep your scoops clean and let commonly accepted, decent behavior govern them. Then your expertise will always be in demand.

Panhandler No. 2 The local politician may have compelling reasons for not announcing his experiment in impoverished living. If you surreptitiously record his spiel, you may harm a worthwhile humanitarian enterprise. You might want, instead, to tell him who you are. Talk to him, explain what you want. Perhaps he will ask you to record but to hold it until he is ready to go public. Then you will have the inside track on the story, and the scoop is still yours.

The secret ingredient in the development of an idea is judgment; you must weigh all outcomes of your action. The younger and keener you are, the easier it is to barge ahead like U.S. Admiral David Farragut, who is reported to have shouted during the Battle of Mobile Bay in 1864: "Damn the torpedoes, full speed ahead!" As long as there are no torpedoes, you are a hero. If there are, your bravado will be judged foolhardy and criminal. That is the point you have to consider. Watch the torpedoes; there are many waiting to sink you along your charted course. Sound judgment will prevent an early demise of your future as a radio journalist.

g. SUMMING UP

Have an idea, develop it, exploit it, find an angle, but stay in control of it. Then, should difficulties develop, examine whether it is worth holding onto. If you decide it is, explore it with all the dedication and drive that you can muster.

2

CHOOSING A FORMAT

You will have to select one radio format in which to present
your idea. It can be broadcast in a variety of ways, in either
a straightforward manner or with artifice.

When you listen to the news, to a sports report, to an
on-the-scene commentary on an historic event, or to a disc
jockey introducing his music, you hear the straightforward
presentation of information. But when information is
combined creatively with sound and music, artifice is
introduced. The more creative radio programs are dramas,
features, docu-dramas, and documentaries. All are similar,
yet they differ in essential ways.

All offer the listener the same characteristics of a good
book that involves you and commands your attention
beyond bedtime. As in a book, a creative radio program, be
it drama, feature, docu-drama, or documentary, offers the
listener the following elements —

- setting,
- characters,
- story, and
- language.

The setting places the action in context; the characters give
the listener a focus; the story carries the listener's interest
and the quality of language determines success or failure.

As well, each type of creative radio program is, technically speaking, a mixture of sounds — speaking and
singing voices, musical instruments, sound effects from
natural sources or synthesizer — that have been recorded
and stored on magnetic tape.

And each finished radio program is broadcast to listeners
within range of transmitters, whether on the shortwave
band, on AM or on FM frequencies, in monophonic or
stereophonic sound.

These are the similarities of radio dramas, features, docu-dramas, and documentaries; but there are differences.

a. RADIO DRAMA AND DOCU-DRAMA

The radio drama is a close cousin of the stage play except that it lacks, perforce, the visuals. Hence the radio drama uses the voice as its principal vehicle to create a setting, a conflict, and a dramatic confrontation. The imaginative use of sound and music provide a substitute for the missing visual elements of a stage play.

Although the radio drama was developed soon after radio was first broadcast, from its early heyday it nearly sank to oblivion. Lately, radio drama has been rediscovered and revitalized.

The radio docu-drama combines drama with documentary, or the thorough examination of the facts related to a topic. A good example is the Canadian Broadcasting Corporation's highly successful radio series, the "Scales of Justice," based on criminal court transcripts but dramatized and recreated by actors.

Radio dramas and docu-dramas depend on the listener's imagination for their effect. When we see a stage play, go to a movie, or switch on the TV set, two of our five principal senses are involved: sight and sound. When you eliminate the sight aspect, the job of entertaining and informing a person is made more challenging. You must create a setting, a scene filled with tension or longing or passion or tenderness or conflict.

The radio drama or docu-drama rises to this task. The listener can sit in a dark room or close the eyes and follow the action created by words and sounds — creaks, screams, laughter, whispers, pieces of music, sudden noises, and even silence.

The listener's capacity for exercising his or her imagination is virtually limitless. Radio drama and docu-drama can create a different dramatic landscape for each listener because each listener has a different experience from which his or her imagination builds a mental image. A door creaks in a different house for each radio drama or docu-drama listener, whereas in a TV drama, only the door on the studio set creaks, leaving nothing to the imagination. The exercise of the imagination is what makes radio dramas and docu-dramas radio forms that continue to flourish.

b. RADIO DOCUMENTARIES AND FEATURES

The word "documentary" is thought to have been originated by a Canadian film pioneer, John Grierson, the man who developed the Canadian National Film Board into a world-renowned institution. Grierson used the term in 1926 to describe *Nanook of the North*, a film by the famous American film director and producer, Robert Flaherty. The term "documentary" was an instant hit in the radio industry and soon had wide use.

The word "feature" originates from "fact," or more precisely, from the Latin *factura* meaning a "making."

But knowing the origins of the terms documentary and feature is less important than knowing what they encompass. A radio feature is often more of an attributed work of art than is a generic radio documentary. Look on the radio documentary as a loaf of bread and on the radio feature as fancy cake.

A radio documentary is a thorough examination of a specific topic, similar to a magazine article, but in a different medium. As a rule, a documentary addresses issues in the realm of public or current affairs. It examines topics of interest to all of us but focuses primarily on contemporary politics, economics, and social concerns. But, just to confuse you, a radio documentary can also shed light on past events, or it can choose a figure of interest and become an aural biography. Radio documentaries can vary in length from 5 to 60 minutes, or they can be multiples, such as a 5-part series of 30 or 60 minutes each. There are few, if any, limits or restrictions.

A radio feature uses a more relaxed, contemplative approach to a subject. It need not be an exhaustive study or an in-depth investigation but rather an assessment, perhaps even a lyrical and descriptive way of telling a story.

The topic of a radio feature often lies just outside the realm of current affairs and is often dedicated to the arts and humanities. Although historical aspects are prominent in features, a contemporary point of view is predominant.

Whether a documentary is on film, video, or radio, similar methods are used to examine the subject. But a film feature differs fundamentally from a radio feature. A feature film is by definition a work of fiction; a radio feature is generally based on factual events, although it may use elements of fiction and drama as well.

c. THE RADIO DOCUMENTARY — TOOL OF A NEW ART FORM

John Grierson said that beyond the news reporters, the magazine writers, and the lecturers, one begins to wander into the world of the documentary proper, into the only world in which documentary can hope to achieve the ordinary virtues of art; that here we pass from plain description of the truth to arrangements, rearrangements, and creative shapings of art. A documentary, he said, is the "creative treatment of actuality." There has never been a better definition.

The raw material, according to Grierson, means nothing in itself; it is only as it is used that it becomes art. If the most important tool in the production of radio documentaries is the microphone, which brings to the hands of the creative artist all the sounds that attend the working of the world, then the question arises: How does that recorded sound become art, rather than just reproduction?

d. A RADIO FEATURE PIONEER

Peter Leonhard Braun of Berlin is widely regarded as a radio feature pioneer. He is often asked to define the radio feature, but he maintains that this is a tiring question because the radio feature is not definable.

At a newspaper, the feature is defined as an enhanced piece of news, a well-prepared and interestingly presented piece of information. In radio, the feature encompasses all modes of presentation; it can involve the listener through the use of drama; it can develop a topic in lengthy, epic curves; it can be a very simple, highly personal reportage; a deadly serious documentation; a highly artistic sound montage; or an entertaining acoustic film. The element connecting all these different forms and techniques is the subject matter.

The feature, Braun does say, must convince listeners that what they are hearing is the truth, that the feature is dealing with real problems and real people.

John Theocharis, head of radio features in the British Broadcasting Corporation's drama department, thinks the radio feature cannot be defined definitively or in an all-encompassing manner. He believes that it has a general definition in which many different possibilities exist; it is consciously a many-faceted world that conveys not only the fact that real subjects are being presented, but also suggests form as well as organization and style.

e. THE CRUX OF THE MATTER

The radio drama, feature, docu-drama, and documentary have the basics in common. All are carefully constructed sound montages recorded on magnetic tape, containing the artifice of speech, sounds, and music. It is in the presentation of these components that they differ.

But whether your idea is presented as a radio drama, feature, docu-drama, or documentary is of secondary importance. The quality of its treatment in radio broadcast form is what is important.

Note: Throughout the rest of this book, whenever the term "documentary" is used, it denotes the radio documentary as well as the radio feature — just to keep things simple. The radio drama and docu-drama, while they demand technical skill similar to the radio documentary and feature, are not treated here.

3

MAKING A PROPOSAL

Sooner or later, you will try to sell your idea for a documentary to a radio producer. It pays off if you are able to put together a proposal that is well reasoned, presents compelling subject matter, offers a fresh approach, is of interest to a wide audience, promises insight into a fascinating area of human endeavor, and, in short, is an irresistible suggestion. A good proposal sells itself.

Your proposal should be more than just an attempt to sell an idea. In chapter 1, you read how an idea grows wings until it flies on its own. Just as an idea needs nurturing and careful development, a proposal needs to be constructed piece by piece.

Below is a discussion of the individual components of a proposal. Not all these components are necessary to a proposal all the time. For shorter radio documentaries, you can keep the proposal short, but it should contain all the right information. For longer program suggestions, the proposal needs to be longer. As a rule, stick to a maximum of three single-spaced typewritten pages. (Turn to the Appendix for sample proposals.)

a. ADDRESS AND DATE

It may appear unnecessary to ask you not to forget your own address at the top of the proposal, but in many years of teaching media students I find that even after I have reminded them to put their name and address on every paper they submit, half of them forget to do so. If you want your proposals to sell your ideas, every letter you write and every page of every proposal you hand in must be clearly identified with your name, address, and the date on which it was submitted.

b. RECIPIENT

It's good policy to address your proposal to a specific person. Ask around, find out from other freelance broadcasters who the most approachable producers are, which ones are prepared to take chances with a tyro and to guide an emerging talent. Then address your proposal specifically to one of those producers. This serves two purposes. First, it won't get handed down the line to someone who has the time to read it, but no clout to make a decision. Second, the recipient will feel flattered that you have put his or her name on your proposal.

Most people tend to dispute their inclination to be swayed by special recognition or a mild form of flattery. By paying homage to this human trait you may tip the scales in your favor. At the same time, do not be ingratiating or subservient, two deadly sins in the world of competitive proposals. Keep your head high, but consider that most people who have achieved status want to be acknowledged properly. Fair enough.

c. TITLE

All media people are busy all the time. Your proposal will arrive in the midst of hectic activity, and if it is to be considered for acceptance, a punchy title can often make the difference between being read and considered or just added to the growing "pending" file — there to gather dust.

Work on the title, spend time on it, write down as many variations as you can think of, then read them aloud to yourself and to friends. How does the title you choose read? Is it original? Or is it a tired expression? Is it short enough? Does it make you want to read on? Does it tell a story in a few words? Does it promise to be exciting? Is it specific? Keep your title short; make it original; focus on one topic only; and make the reader want to carry on reading.

In 1976, I proposed a two-hour feature on "The Last Run of the Orient Express." The title described the content; it had precise focus; it told a story; it promised to take the listener on a famous train trip (it did when the feature was done); there was the promise of mystery; the element of nostalgia was touched because it was the train's last run. All the elements of an irresistible proposal were summarized in the title.

The proposal was accepted immediately. All the signals were set right. How could anyone not want to listen to the sad demise of this train of spies and adventurers, the train that transported the arms dealer Sir Basil Zaharoff and served as the topic for three famous novels and many other books?

Find a title that summarizes an excellent topic, and you've got a foot in the door.

d. PRÉCIS

Again, keep in mind that the person who might buy your proposal is busy, so it is wise to condense your program idea to a one- or two-sentence précis, or overview, that can be read at a glance. If this précis is composed just right and the subject matter interests the potential buyer, then the rest of your proposal will be studied and considered.

Next to the title, the précis is the most important selling tool of your proposal. Put yourself in the shoes of the person who might want to buy your idea. You want to pull this person in, line by line, to the point where your telephone will ring, or the post office will deliver a contract.

e. TOPIC DESCRIPTION

Write your topic description as a story. A dry list of what you hope to achieve can undo what a good title and précis have done. Tell the story of your program; get the reader involved and interested. Charge them with your enthusiasm.

Don't state that your proposal is unique, that anyone who wouldn't buy it is a fool. The topic description will be evidence of that, and such bombastic reasoning is too easily resisted.

Enthusiasm for the topic is harder to ignore. But remember to keep the church in the village, as the German proverb goes, which means to keep a rein on your flamboyance. Toe the line between modesty and self-assurance. Keep the topic description short as well, because you have only three pages maximum for your proposal.

f. RESEARCH

Everyone loves to give a contract to a competent professional who doesn't forget vital deadlines and knows how to do research. Show them that you know the ropes.

First, inform them of the kind of sources you will research for your documentary. This will help convince them that you are familiar with the subject matter.

Second, tell them how you will go about conducting your research. Don't supply details; give just enough information to make the point. Once you have become an old hand, you will know which road to take (see chapter 5, Doing the Research).

g. INTERVIEWS

The list of planned interviews is an indispensable part of your proposal. It shows the potential buyer that you have spent time on your proposal and that you have lined up some good people to interview. Your interviewing the "right" people is often the key to a proposal being accepted. If you don't know specific names — as happened in the Orient Express proposal — list the kind of people you hope to interview.

As you list names, start with the most impressive ones; give their occupations and locations. If the interviewees are local, you should have no problem lining up meetings; if they are elsewhere, suggest feasible ways of interviewing them, whether it be by your traveling to see them, interviewing them by telephone and recording their answers (not so good because of poor sound quality), or making arrangements with a radio station where your speaking partners live for a studio-to-studio link. Potential buyers of your program idea will appreciate your giving them options, which shows that you are cost-conscious on their behalf.

h. TRAVEL

The urge to travel is overpowering for many people. But when you make your proposal, don't suggest expensive trips to a foreign country just because you'd like to go there. Be aware that your deskbound potential buyer, who would love to travel too, will see through your travel suggestions. Keep them to a minimum unless — as in the case of the Orient Express proposal — travel is the object, or the subject matter is identified with and located in a specific area.

Then suggest low cost travel methods: air charter, local buses and trains, and small hotels. Research the travel costs and give a lump sum total. You can offer details for later discussion.

i. YOUR FEE AND EXPENSES

There are direct and indirect costs connected with every proposal for a program. The radio station bears the indirect costs. You cause extra direct costs, so keep them down.

Your fee will either be stipulated according to a collective agreement or set individually following no clear rules. Find out what the practice is. Write or telephone the appropriate broadcast union (in the United States, the Writers Union of America East or West) and in Canada, the Alliance of Canadian Cinema, Television and Radio Artists (ACTRA) for their fee schedule. In some jurisdictions, you may find that other unions who are not normally associated with broadcasting are the bargaining agents; in that case, ask the local labor federation for information.

Where there are no clear-cut union fees, you must step more gingerly. There are always established practices, and finding out what they are may take a little diplomacy. Take established broadcast journalists into your confidence and ask them to share information from their experience. Some may refuse, while others may co-operate. Or, go to the producer who may buy your proposal and enquire whether fees are fixed or negotiable.

Either way, don't let yourself be persuaded to settle for a low fee because "we cannot afford to pay you more." That kind of argument is specious, and if you accept it you will end up working for a pittance, which is bad for business, bad for your self-esteem, and bad for your livelihood. Insist on proper payment. If you cannot reach an amiable agreement, walk away. Better no contract than being grossly underpaid and exploited.

Keep your expenses flexible. Consider that you may have to offer an honorarium to an expert interviewee, but try to avoid this kind of thing as it adds to the expenses. You can control your other expenses by judicious manipulation. Then suggest a reasonable lump sum estimate and offer to supply details on request. Don't be greedy; show that you are trying to keep expenses down.

j. COMPLETION DATE

Be realistic. When handing in your proposal try to juggle two imponderables: the broadcast medium's schedule and your own time. Tell your potential buyers what they most likely want to hear as a completion date, but don't jeopardize your program by promising short delivery when you know it cannot be done by then. The more programs you put together, the more surely you can guess the completion date.

As a rule, deadlines are good, because they make you apply yourself. But an unrealistic deadline can cause 18-hour workdays, create great stress, and likely contribute to a poorly produced program. The deadline is a desperately important factor, and you had better come to terms with it.

One famous radio producer works to deadline with minutes to spare. That is poor judgment and bad workmanship. This producer once reeled off a just completed one-hour documentary onto a takeup reel already half full. As the high-speed tape recorder rewound the tape, the producer walked away to do something else. Suddenly the takeup reel was full and the excess tape shot into the room. Four people had to help unravel the twisted mess; they finished two minutes before air time.

That kind of disaster is avoidable. Suggest a completion date and, after you receive a contract for the assignment, revise it if you realize it is too tight.

k. QUALIFICATIONS

Until you have built a reputation for being able to deliver quality programs every time, you are faced with an uphill struggle. You must tell the potential buyers of your program proposal that you can deliver what you have promised.

But the broadcast world is full of skeptics. The question "Can we trust XYZ to deliver?" is not idle. Too many inexperienced freelancers suggest too many raw proposals to too many potential buyers. As a result, the buyers have become wary.

You may consider letting your potential buyer listen to one of your productions, but there are two pitfalls to this. First, you may not have a sample program that is good enough for the big time (everyone has to start somewhere). Second, listening to sample programs demands the potential buyer's precious time. In most cases, attaching a sample program to your proposal is a waste of time.

Reputation is your biggest qualification, but if you cannot offer reputation, offer a solidly constructed, intelligent, thoughtful, and nonexperimental proposal.

l. FOLLOW-UP

After the proposal has arrived at its destination, give it a week and then follow up with a telephone call or, much better, a visit to the producer. Try to avoid a time when you know the producer will be busy. Ask the receptionist or secretary the best time to call or visit. Also, if you can, find out what mood the person is in that day. Be straightforward with the receptionist or secretary; tell him or her how important it is for you to have your proposal accepted.

When and if you are able to see the producer, don't, under any circumstances, tell him or her you are desperate for work. No one likes a hard luck story. Be positive; tell the producer more about your proposal; add any new facts that might strengthen your case. But know when to be quiet and listen.

Observe your buyer closely. Some want to dazzle you with their own pet projects. If so, listen politely, but bring the discussion back to your proposal.

Finally, try to get a commitment, preferably in writing. Get them to issue a contract, and sign it.

4

GETTING ORGANIZED

Organizing your thoughts, your skills, your attitude, and your time is of paramount importance to your success as a radio journalist. That's the first leg on which to stand.

The second leg is to be self-disciplined, to get going in the morning, to do everything you have planned, to finish every project, to avoid procrastination, and to realize that being sloppy and disorganized is not a creative way to work.

I have witnessed too many potentially excellent radio journalists who failed because they could not get organized and exercise self-discipline. But how do you do it?

Most people cannot get organized in the abstract. They need what the French call an *aide memoire* — notes to trigger action. It is crucial to write everything down, to keep your notes available, and to refer to them all the time. Without knowing what to look for, and where to look, you cannot hope to keep your deadlines. Therefore, getting organized is not a luxury, it is a necessity.

The following steps will help you get organized.

a. DEFINE YOUR PROJECT

What is it you want to do with the idea you have developed? Who will want to hear what you have created? What is the best length and format? In what time span can you hope to accomplish the project? Be realistic, not vague when you answer these questions.

Make sure you can find the people to be interviewed; check the cost, travel time, and production time. In short, mentally run through the entire production. If you are a novice, double the time just to give yourself a safety margin.

Once you set these parameters, look at your potential ideas one by one. Then choose, reject, and discard.

b. LAY OUT THE COMPONENTS

Have you been given a contract for the kind of money you want and need? Revise it now because it is bad form to go back and ask for more travel and expense money at a later stage.

Have you lined up all the people involved in your project? Are they available when you need them? Are all the basic questions you must ask your interviewees noted down and accessible?

Have you checked your hardware? Is the tape recorder working at the right speed? Have you cleaned it? Are the batteries fresh? Do you have a spare set of batteries? Are all the cables recording properly? Do you have all the paraphernalia such as windsocks, cradle suspensions, pistol grips, T-bars, patchcords, extension cords, carrying case, spare cassettes or tapes, and headphones? (See chapter 7, Selecting Your Recording Hardware.) Do you have a small multipurpose tool, such as a Swiss army knife?

Do you have your travel itinerary? Has everyone been notified? Do you have a notebook and relevant research notes? A letter of introduction? (In some foreign countries, it's advisable to have a written document with you certifying you are who you are.) Do you have all the telephone numbers you need?

None of these questions are extraneous; all are vital.

c. DETERMINE YOUR APPROACH

There are so many ways to tackle a project. Generally, though, if you appreciate the setting of the landscape and the people you visit, you will step with care. Realize that small towns or villages have different attitudes toward a big city radio journalist. Your methods may not be accepted.

When you enter other countries, study their priorities, their social habits, their way of doing things, and you will avoid much trouble. Again, realize that people with microphones and cameras are not always welcome in times of trouble.

For example, when I was determining my approach for the radio documentary, "The Last Run of the Orient Express," I wrote to all the state railroads, asking for permission to interview railroad officials. In every case, the railroads responded enthusiastically and gave unstinting help.

But when it came to implement that approach, the project nearly came to grief. The Turkish Army wanted to forbid my radio team to interview anyone outside the railroad station. The reason soon became clear. On May 1, 1977, when our radio team was getting ready to leave Istanbul, thousands of workers amassed near Taksim Square on Labor Day. During the rally some 38 people were shot dead and hundreds were injured by sniper fire from the rooftops. Our radio team escaped unharmed, but the reason for the army's reluctance to let us roam freely was established: Trouble had been expected, and no government likes to have foreign news teams record such events.

If you have doubts whether the area and the people you will visit are going to be friendly, be careful, but also try to find a resident who can facilitate your approach.

d. MAKE A FLOW CHART

It helps to prepare a flow chart showing all the components of your project progressing in tandem toward completion, with time as the governing factor. This flow chart should contain the central idea, the project, the approach, the people concerned (interview partners, producer, technicians, others involved peripherally), the deadline, the production schedule, financing, travel, research, hardware (whether or not other pieces are needed), and any other components that could show or endanger the project. Sample #1 shows an example of a flow chart.

Your flow chart need not be elaborate or complicated. As long as you have jotted down somewhere, preferably in graphic form, all the components of your project, you are sure not to miss one. Do not rely on your memory alone; use organized notes.

e. SET A SCHEDULE

Your schedule should be part of the flow chart. As a general rule, planning a series of interviews and recordings in different locations always takes longer than anticipated. Schedule these events keeping minor and major mishaps in mind. Leave much earlier for an assignment, for instance, than you would assume is necessary.

Most people you interview will be short of time. Being late for an interview often kills it for good. The professional always leaves early enough to be five minutes ahead of time. Politicians, business people, officials, professionals, academics — none of them wants to wait for you. There is a German proverb that says "Punctuality is the politeness of kings."

It also makes sense to never miss a deadline.

f. ESTABLISH A WORK PATTERN

The rhythm of an operation determines the smoothness of the finished project. But rhythm does not mean routine, just as being methodical does not mean being pedantic. It simply makes sense to establish a work pattern that begins with A and ends with Z. The secret of a work pattern is not to let yourself be bound by a straitjacket but to operate so smoothly that all your energies are directed toward the project.

If you follow that kind of pattern, you eventually will outrun the most hectic colleague who works at breakneck speed but is disorganized and misses the deadline after all.

SAMPLE #1
RADIO DOCUMENTARY FLOW CHART

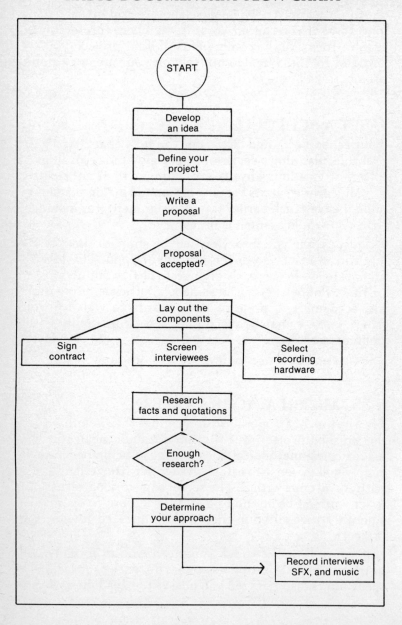

START

Develop
an idea

Define your
project

Write a
proposal

Proposal
accepted?

Lay out the
components

Sign
contract

Screen
interviewees

Select
recording
hardware

Research
facts and quotations

Enough
research?

Determine
your approach

Record interviews
SFX, and music

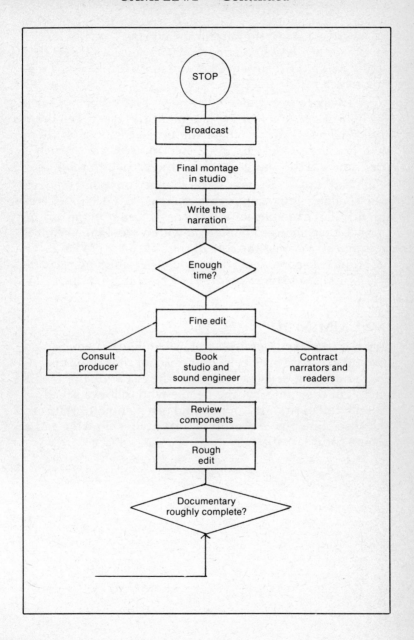

g. CHECK THE OVERVIEW

From time to time, step back from your project and take a look at what's going on. Although your ideas may make it to the project stage, they aren't always ripe. Any number of people connected with your project may miss an aspect that would make the difference between an average and a distinguished radio program.

One way to overview your project is to rethink it with the help of outsiders whose judgment you trust. Tell them the concept and what stage the project is at. Ask them whether they would be interested in listening to such a program. Do they agree with your approach to the topic?

The objective is to stand back, change your point of view, and challenge all your premises. Use "What if . . ." frequently. For example, what if the basic assumptions for the project have changed while you weren't looking? What if your questions miss the core of the argument? What if the story has disappeared while you were pursuing a side story? Catch mistakes before they ruin an ambitious production.

h. SUMMING UP

Try not to make the mistake of assuming that you can do an entire feature project in your head, or that being organized and being self-disciplined is the mark of the media hack. On the contrary, the people who follow a schedule usually finish first. It can't be said often enough: Without self-discipline a media professional invites disaster and a dismal future.

5

DOING THE RESEARCH

You are now at the point in your project where the good times begin. You are about to do the research. For many people, researching a subject is quintessential bliss. Some authors and journalists are so intoxicated with research that they never finish, postponing the day when all the material gathered has to be sifted, selected, discarded and fashioned into a book, an article, or a radio program. You will not do that. If you do, you will have a good time in the poorhouse.

Instead learn where to look for facts, how to look, and when to stop looking. Move swiftly, find the right source, copy down whatever facts are needed, and go to work assembling the program.

Here are the steps to researching efficiently and effectively and to avoiding the pitfalls of excessive investigation.

a. METHODOLOGY

First decide what research method you will use. There are choices — some cheap, some very expensive.

If you have a computer, a modem, a printer, and a few hundred dollars to spare, you can research electronically. You can access a variety of on-line information services. Find out about them through your public library.

The preferred source of information is a university or public library. There you can find books, magazines, reference sources, newspaper files, and helpful librarians who specialize in research. If you have winning ways about you and can get the generally overworked library staff interested in your project, they will bring you tome after tome of facts.

Another method is to ask questions and follow your inspiration. That is what private eyes do all the time in mystery novels, and if they are good, they find what they are looking for. If you have bloodhound instincts, you may prefer this kind of primary research. Otherwise, try the library.

b. WHERE TO LOOK

Your choices in a public library or archive are almost too wide. As a rule, it is easier to begin with encyclopedias, which will give you a quick overview of how much work you are facing.

If your project is vast, narrow the subject, until you can focus on a specific area. Avoid irrelevant detail, a task not as easy as it sounds.

Then, establish the boundaries of your research project: Where will the most concentrated accumulation of data be located? In books, magazines, newspapers, government reports, dissertations, or reference books? Is the information on microfilm or microfiche? Talk to the librarians about possible sources.

Here are some helpful hints for extrapolating the information in different sources:

Books and magazines If there are more than a few sentences per page, make photocopies. The money spent is less than the time used to write information down. Look for a periodical index to magazines to save more time.

Newspapers If there are clippings, photocopy them so they fill as much of a page as possible. If there are microfilms or microfiche, request copies even though you may have to wait a day. Sometimes making notes is faster, depending on your schedule.

Old records Libraries and archives often have invaluable old government records and reports. Sometimes they can disclose the reason for a contemporary event.

As you dig through these sources, try to detect an emerging story. Apply your instincts, as did Carl Bernstein and Bob Woodward, the two *Washington Post* reporters who pursued the Watergate affair.

Use your instinct, tenacity, perseverance, endurance, and patience. These five qualities serve you well in research, and also on the trail of a story.

c. WHO TO ASK

Ask questions of anybody who knows something you want to know. You can find these people everywhere. If you are looking for an expert in a particular field, approach the local professional association, or ask any particular professional. For example, if you need a legal expert, call the law society or bar association or try making direct contact with a lawyer.

Another option is to track down someone who practices some specialty as a hobby. Keep in mind that professional experts sometimes are short of time and might even charge for their expertise; on the other hand, amateur experts will often spend hours with you, giving freely of their time and effort to help your research.

You can start by looking in the Yellow Pages under organizations, churches, service clubs, social clubs, ethnic groups, or any kind of association that could possibly be connected with your topic. Contact the organization and go from there.

If you own a computer, access on-line information services or dial your local Bulletin Board Service (BBS) at no cost, and perhaps get referred to another computer user group or BBS elsewhere that has all the names you need.

d. PERSEVERE

Perseverance is one of the qualities of a good researcher. But there will be many times when your research gets stuck. When that happens, change the ambience. Go for a walk. Stop reading one source and switch to another. Chop wood. Eat a meal. Do anything to break the pattern that led to a mental block.

If that doesn't work, discard your previous approach. Assume that you have finished the research, that your approach hasn't worked, and that you must rethink everything. Then do that. Change direction, rethink the focus, and alter the approach.

Suddenly the story will come together. If you had given up when things weren't going right, you would have missed the story, lost confidence, and perhaps moved to another line of work. Stick to your story. If the basic premise is sound, persevere.

e. WHEN TO STOP LOOKING

After a few days or weeks at the most, go through your accumulated research, and start looking for a pattern. You may have enough information to go with what you have.

Check the following to avoid over-researching your subject:

- Translate the amount of time you will have to tell your story into pages of print. As a general guideline, it takes two to three minutes to read aloud one page.
- Render your projected program time into word blocks and compare the available space with the dozens of pages of research you have gathered. Then ask yourself how on earth you will ever succeed in boiling it down to size.
- Keep in mind that figures and facts are even more dull when mentioned on the air than when printed on a page. Stay away from them. They can give you background for your subject, but are not for direct quotation.

When your research is complete, you will want to rewrite its salient points in your own language and tell the condensed version to the world. So take stock of where you are in your research; stop if you feel you might have enough. You will, in fact, have too much.

f. HOW TO SIFT FACTS

Now that all the data are in front of you, you must sift the facts. Choose and discard, but never throw anything away — not even when your project has become a program and you have gone on to bigger things. I have been able to reuse much of my original research many years after the event. Once I thought that one particular piece of information was worthless after the project had been realized so I threw the notes away. Sure enough, several years later I was asked to provide the same notes and had to go out, grinding my teeth, to repeat the entire research process.

As you sift through your research, make three piles:

- The prime-time stuff (what you want to save)
- The also-ran stuff (what might be upgraded later, if necessary)
- The no-no stuff (what seems irrelevant)

Keep all three piles in descending order, but allot all notes to the correct pile. You will find that you will need information from all three as your project changes or a side issue attains higher importance.

But how do you determine what goes into which pile? Trial and error will teach you. Because you have kept all your data, any errors in dividing the research can be corrected later.

As the years go by and your files begin to bulge, go through your research and discard the bad stuff. But remember, always keep the good and the so-so, because initial research is like working capital. Hundreds of companies are in business to sell information. We live in an age that appears to want more and more facts as food for enterprise. The data you have amassed in your files (on paper or on computer disc) are valuable property. And they are yours. You found them.

6

FINDING PEOPLE TO INTERVIEW

By now you have a contract for your radio documentary, you've completed your research, and you are ready to interview — to put your microphone where someone else's mouth is, so to speak. In this chapter, you will learn to line up an interview; then in the next two chapters, how to use your equipment to record your interviewee's voice at its best.

But first, whom do you interview? Interviewees are your most important source of facts and opinions in a radio project. While your research is also important, it must be balanced with the spontaneity of a number of interviews.

For the "Last Run of the Orient Express" documentary I asked the state railroads to provide experts along the way. I also lined up local authors and journalists working along the Orient Express's route. These were the professionals I interviewed; they spoke from a technical point of view. As well I interviewed the passengers on the train, who were my amateurs; they provided color and unexpected comic relief. The amateurs I could not screen beforehand; the professionals, I could.

The best procedure is to try to talk with interviewees before deciding whether they are knowledgeable, believable, authoritative, warm, fluent, and well-spoken.

As you start making your telephone calls to people you want to interview, assess how they might do in an interview before you formally ask them. Make notes you can refer to later. You may expect a person with an illustrious name, for example, to be a natural, only to find that he or she speaks poorly and is completely unsuitable. If so, bow out gracefully.

a. PROFESSIONALS

Professionals are people who have a sure grasp of their subject matter, are used to speaking publicly, have been interviewed before, and know how it is done. Politicians, senior civil servants, academics, administrators, and upper echelon executives all fall into this category. Generally speaking, professionals are the easiest people to interview because they have done it so many times before. They understand what you want, and they often give you what you need.

However, you cannot assume that professionals are good interviewees just because they are experienced. Many speak professional gobbledygook, or jargon. Unfortunately, you have to record it; you can always edit their statements when you're putting all the pieces together.

Even though you may be dissatisfied with an interviewee, use your common sense and be polite at all times. Respect your interviewee's status and the ego that often accompanies it.

Also, use the correct terms of address. For example, you would not address a question to a bishop with "Say, bishop, what do you think of . . . ?" Rather, you would ask "Your Excellency, what do you think of . . . ?" Steer the middle course between being rude and being obsequious. It doesn't cost you anything to acknowledge rank and to be polite, and it can mean the difference between an adequate interview and a top-notch one.

b. AMATEURS

Whatever your topic, you will probably be able to find amateur experts who are willing to be interviewed. Literally, the word "amateur" means "a lover," who might be a lover of words, facts, or history.

Any of these people could serve as an interviewee for your documentary. If they are well versed in their respective discipline, and if they can translate their knowledge into descriptive passages, they can be interviewed.

On the Orient Express, I met three elderly women from Ohio who were playing amateur detectives, re-enacting Hercule Poirot and Miss Marple, the Agatha Christie sleuths. None of the three had ever spoken publicly, but they talked rather well and amusingly about their love for trains and mystery novels, including some of their own adventures on the Orient Express. The triple interview was a success and I used it in the two-hour feature as counterpoint to expert interviews.

Be on constant lookout for such so-called amateurs, who quite often turn out better than the pros. But if you find someone whose expertise is essential for the success of your project, and he or she is a poor interview, record the answers and later transcribe or paraphrase the statements in your written narration.

As well, if your amateur expert, like some professionals, uses such specialized language that the average listener will not be able to follow, first, record the statement; then try to understand what was said or seek someone who does understand; and later edit the statement.

c. VOICES

The absence of visual focus in radio means the listener must concentrate not only on what is said, but how it is said, to gain meaning. A well-modulated voice is therefore important.

The best interviewees use rising and falling inflections, speak in complete sentences, accentuate in the right places, and have rich, warm voices expressing their humanity. They have radiophonically acceptable voices; that is, when they are heard on radio, they can be understood and they speak clearly.

In contrast, those interviewees who whine, who speak nasally or so sibilantly they defy the abilities of the sound engineer who must compensate for them, or who have speech patterns that make listeners nervous or disgusted, are not the best choice. Neither are speakers who ramble, drone on, and never inflect their voices. They will put listeners to sleep.

If you line up an interviewee whose message is important, but whose voice sounds terrible, or has such a strong accent the average listener would have trouble understanding, paraphrase. Quote the speaker in your narration, incorporating the gist of the speaker's comments.

d. DICTION

Diction is what makes a good speaking voice intelligible. Some speakers, despite all the rich timbre and the beautiful inflection, slur their sentences, swallow their g's, and forget to complete sentences because they speak quickly and without control. Such speakers cannot be understood without straining.

Professionals who realize how important their verbal image is to their careers often take lessons in elocution and learn how to construct a sentence, to pronounce words correctly, and to be understood.

Watch for the mispronunciation of little-used words that most people see written but rarely hear spoken. I will never forget the professional radio announcer who said "From this moment on, everything went awry." He pronounced it "aw-ree," rather than "a-rye." Don't let such poor diction slip into your interviews. You are a guardian of the language by virtue of the fact that it is your sole tool; you have an obligation to treat it with respect.

e. THOSE UMs AND AHs

When you discuss setting up an interview with people, listen closely to how they say what they say. Will their voices withstand the distortion of a microphone? How many *um*s and *ah*s do they use? Do they talk like this: "Mr.... ah... Hesse, I want... um... I was thinking... ah... could we... um... maybe try... ah... um... anyway, next week... or... um... perhaps next... ah... month . . ." and so on.

This is not an exaggerated example of how many people talk. Listen to a one-sided telephone conversation. The use of *um*s and *ah*s is so widespread that someone could make a mint teaching people to avoid the habit of trying to bridge silence with unessential sounds. You will begin to hate *um*s and *ah*s when you have to edit them out of an otherwise brilliant interview. (See chapter 12, How to Pick, Save, and Discard). If you can, say thanks but no thanks to a user of excessive *um*s and *ah*s.

You may also prefer not to interview a stutterer.

f. LOCATION

Carefully consider where you locate an interview. Most people prefer to be interviewed in their offices or their homes. Public places are too noisy and should be avoided.

Half the battle of doing a successful interview is to relax an uptight or nervous speaker. If nothing else helps, pin a lapel microphone on their shirt, tie or blouse, and make them forget that they are being recorded. Take off your headphones, and soon they will forget they are speaking into a mike.

Invite your interviewee to sit closer to you, so you get a good quality voice recording. Place the furniture according to your needs, not the way your interviewee would like to sit. In an office, speakers often prefer to barricade themselves behind their desks because they feel safe there. Extricate them from behind and bring them out in front of the desk. Place your chair parallel but facing their chair, so that you will sit side by side but facing each other. This position allows you to rest the arm supporting your microphone on the arm of your chair, while holding it below the speaker's mouth. (See chapter 8, Using a Microphone.)

In a home, select the dining room table with its upright chairs rather than a couch or an easy chair. People get tired more easily in a slouched position; their attention wanders. Also you can't hold the microphone close enough for good recording quality, which is no more than one foot away.

At the table, seat your interviewee to your right or left side so you are at a right angle from him or her. That way you are both comfortable and your microphone arm is supported.

g. HONORARIA

Sometimes your chosen interviewees will want to be paid. This usually happens with freelance or self-employed media people who consider their expertise part of their potential income. In those cases, honoraria must be agreed on before the interview.

Academics, administrators, politicians, scientists, or people who are being paid while they talk to you, should not expect an honorarium. If they demand it, negotiate and argue your point. Amateurs almost never ask to be paid because they like to be heard on their pet project and they give their expertise willingly and freely.

If your interviewees insist on being paid and you have no budget, or if they demand too much money, walk away from the interview. But ideally, settle these details before you see them.

h. SAFEGUARDING

It is sometimes the case that interviewees whose statements are edited claim you have quoted them out of context. If you have conscientiously edited their statements, and you feel sure you have not altered the intent of the statement, you have little to worry about.

Usually these people claim they were quoted out of context when what they said creates a furor and they are looking for a scapegoat. That is dishonest and is the fear of many journalists because there is little defense to this charge short of going to court. The best way to avoid such confrontation is to eliminate inflammatory remarks unless other sources corroborate them.

7

SELECTING YOUR RECORDING HARDWARE

In a time when new recording hardware is constantly being developed and perfected, it is difficult to pinpoint state-of-the-art technology. Changes are frequent and recorders are often superseded. Sometimes it seems obsolescence is built into the hardware. However, at the time of writing, all the innovative methods of sound recording are happening outside broadcast media, so you can count on a number of years when portable recording technology will remain at the current level.

The following discussion of hardware is neither highly technical nor is it complete. But it should help you get started.

a. MONO OR STEREO?

It used to be simple. Monophonic sound was broadcast on AM radio and stereophonic sound on FM. Now some AM radio stations and television stations can broadcast in stereo.

Although you may work for an AM radio station that is still broadcasting in mono, acquaint yourself with stereo production techniques. Your radio documentary should be in stereo since it can always be broadcast in mono; a mono production cannot be broadcast in stereo.

Stereo is state-of-the-art sound. It is simply an improvement over mono, or hi-fi sound, which was able to provide listeners with excellent loudspeakers and headphones that produced unadulterated and undistorted sound. Stereo adds another dimension to the sound environment and makes you feel as if you are sitting in the middle of an orchestra; mono sound keeps you separated from the source.

Mono sound is recorded with one microphone, or more if a sound mixer is used (see section d. below). Stereo sound is recorded with two or more microphones on two or more separate tracks. Each track reproduces the location of the specific sound the microphone has captured.

Try the following experiment. Listen to your environment with one ear — in mono — then with both ears — in stereo. That will demonstrate the power and the beauty of stereo more than any technical explanation.

b. RECORDERS

In tape recorders you have a choice of reel-to-reel, cassette, and video recorders. Each has its best application, but reel-to-reel recorders continue to be predominant in the broadcast studio for a number of reasons.

1. Reel-to-reel

Even though reel-to-reel recorders and tape are cumbersome to use, they refuse to be superannuated. And even though you have to take the time and effort to secure the open ends to prevent the tape unravelling, and to manually wind the tape around the record-playback-erase heads, reel-to-reel recorders are the workhorse of the studio.

Reel-to-reel recorders remain in use because of their sound quality. They use quarter-inch tape, which has more area on which the sound can be recorded, and they also record at higher speeds than cassette recorders.

An audio cassette is usually recorded and played back at a speed of 1-⅞ inches per second (ips), but audio tape for professional applications is usually recorded at a minimum of 7-½ ips. Other speeds range from 15/16 ips to 1-⅞ ips, 3-¾ ips, 15 ips and 30 ips. The slowest speed, 15/16 ips, is good only for an audio log of everything broadcast. The fastest speed, 30 ips, is used for commercial music recordings.

Sound recorded at higher speeds is better because the longer the area of audio tape on which the sound is recorded, the better the fidelity, the less tape hiss, the greater the definition, and the higher the sound's presence.

More tape runs by the recording head at higher speeds, thus tape recorded at speeds greater than 1-⅞ ips will play back better sound than tape recorded at speeds of 1-⅞ ips.

Similarly, more recording area runs past the recording head with wider tape, thus quarter-inch tape will play back better sound than cassette tape.

Another reason for using reel-to-reel recorders is that you can make a clean, precise cut in the open reel tape. Such editing is not possible with cassette tape, although you can edit cassettes electronically, but that is a slow and imprecise method.

A reel-to-reel recorder can record in half-track or quarter-track stereo. It can also use two-track or four-track tape. Unfortunately the terms half-track and two-track, quarter-track and four-track, although linguistically opposed, are technically identical. Both sets refer to separate sound tracks recorded simultaneously on one stretch of tape. Half-track means that the tape has been divided into a left and a right track; two tracks means there are a left and a right track on one tape (the industry standard is to assign the upper track to the left channel and the lower track to the right). Quarter-track means there are two left and two right tracks on one tape, but alternately; tracks one and three are on the right track and tracks two and four are on the left. (See Figure #1.)

For professional applications, two-track recordings are recommended because they use the entire width of the tape, which can be recorded in only one direction. Two track or half-track stereo gives better sound because it, again, uses wider tracks. However it is costly because you use twice as much tape as with four-track, or quarter-track, stereo.

But as a professional, you have no choice. Editing a quarter-track audio tape with a razor blade is impossible because you would also cut the two tracks running in the opposite direction.

When selecting a reel-to-reel recorder you have the options of a portable or a stationary recorder. Portable means it can be carried over your shoulder and be powered by dry batteries; stationary means it can be carried but needs a main connection for power.

FIGURE #1
TRACK POSITIONS

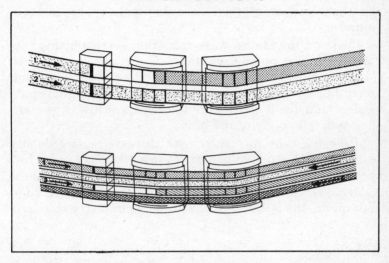

There are broadcast quality portable tape recorders available in mono and stereo. Film production companies and broadcasting companies use them extensively. The cost of these portable reel-to-reel tape recorders is relatively high, as they can cost as much as US $10,000.

Many radio broadcasters use a portable cassette recorder, then transfer the sound to a stationary reel-to-reel. They keep the half-track stereo tape recorders in the studio for editing and assembling the master tape.

If you choose to use a reel-to-reel only as an editing machine, it must be sturdy. It can have either full-track mono recording and playback heads, two-track stereo recording and playback heads, or even two-track mono heads. All these tape recorders are usable as long as they have an "instant stop" button, sometimes called an "edit" button, that does not pull the tape away from the playback head.

2. Cassette

The portable, high quality cassette recorder market is dominated by SONY. The most popular recorder comes in both mono and stereo, but most radio stations prefer the more expensive mono model, because it can survive rough handling more readily than the more fragile stereo model. Further, news or interviews are almost always broadcast in mono.

Insist on the Dolby noise reduction system in any cassette recorder you buy, whether it is portable or stationary (a cassette deck). You engage the Dolby system when you record or use playback, and this ensures the highest possible sound quality with a minimum of tape hiss. The manuals will tell you why and how.

Take the time to research which cassettes are quality products. I have found that it isn't wise to save a few pennies by buying inferior products. For stereo, I found the SONY "Walkman Professional" a state-of-the-art recorder. For mono, the SONY "TCM5000" is the industry standard.

3. Video

Video provides an alternative to expensive portable reel-to-reel tape recorders. The sound tracks on a portable hi-fi half-inch video cassette recorder (VCR) or on the new 8 mm digital format video cassette recorders can record superb stereo sound for up to 12 hours on one cassette, at a fraction of the cost. However, the half-inch and 8 mm VCRs are developed to record images as well as sound, so using them for sound only is still more expensive than cassette tape. For most applications, the sound quality provided by portable audio cassette recorders will be adequate for today's radio stations.

Video recorders do provide the option of two dimensions. You could be making a radio program while working on a video production. Although such dual enterprises are rare, they do exist; then a VCR will provide you with both images and sound of good quality.

My recommendations are that you buy a portable cassette recorder and dub the sound later to quarter-inch tape, either on your own reel-to-reel tape recorder or at a radio or sound production studio.

4. New technology

In the short space of 25 years, from 1961 to 1986, sound recording technology has undergone innovative, drastic, and spectacular improvements.

In 1961, when I started my broadcast career, the only portable machines available were the old crank-up tape recorders with a running time of three minutes. After that, the first heavy, battery powered, open-reel portable tape recorders came on the market. These recorders, especially those manufactured in Europe, immediately set the standard for many years.

Then, light-weight, battery-powered portable cassette recorders were introduced, and soon Japan dominated the field. Although these clever little machines were admirable and the idea of miniaturizing the electronic hardware was exciting, the technology resembled the horse-and-buggy stage of sound recording.

By the late seventies, technology had been perfected to the current state of the art, and now these small cassette recorders are so sophisticated, so accurate, so durable, so dependable, and so inexpensive to buy and operate that the early days of portable sound equipment are like a distant nightmare. As this is written, new breakthroughs in this technology are not anticipated, and the fidelity of these machines is good enough to satisfy the most finicky sound engineers.

But everywhere in the world there are geniuses at work, developing new technology for the consumer market. Although digital sound recording and other newfangled technologies have been developed, chances are that the current state-of-the-art portable cassette recorders will be around for many years to come.

Despite all the technological advances, the cassette tape format has not changed since it was invented. A similar cassette format, the microcassette, has been developed, but the quality is not up to broadcast standards. Its main value is its usefulness for dictation or as a notebook.

The size and weight of a full feature, state-of-the-art portable stereo cassette recorder have been reduced to the absolute minimum. Further refinements will no doubt be added but presumably without changing the principle. A similar future can be predicted for the open-reel portable and the reel-to-reel studio tape recorders. They will be further refined, but generally stay unchanged.

It appears, then, that high quality portable recording technology is going to be with us for a number of years. You can expect a solid, well-built tape recorder to work for many years if you maintain it well and treat it with the respect a precision tool demands. It is unlikely you will have to replace an outdated recorder with a costly new model for a long time.

The new digital technology need not frighten you into buying a new machine. To use an analogy, to get from point A to B safely a driver does not need the latest model sports car. A 10-year-old jalopy in good repair will get you there just as safely and quickly. The same applies for recording technology. As long as the product — sound — conforms to current standards of broadcast quality, there is no need to buy the latest equipment. You may, therefore, safely assume that for the remainder of the decade, you will not have to spend thousands of dollars to upgrade your recording equipment.

c. THE MICROPHONE

There are two kinds of microphones for the professional broadcaster in the field: the dynamic mike and the condenser mike.

1. Dynamic microphones

The dynamic mike is a sturdy, reliable, virtually indestructible instrument developed for outdoor use, on the road, in wind and rain, and in hot or cold climates. It is ideal if you need a microphone that must work under adverse conditions.

The dynamic microphone comes in two basic configurations: omnidirectional and unidirectional (cardioid). (See Figure #2). The omnidirectional microphone is good only in enclosed spaces without too much ambient noise. It picks up sound from everywhere, and in that sense it resembles the human ear. For news conferences and interviews with more than one person, it can be of great value.

The unidirectional microphone has a narrower acoustic focus and excludes much of the ambient noise in an enclosed space. It is good for isolating interview partners in a crowd.

FIGURE #2
DYNAMIC MICROPHONE CONFIGURATIONS

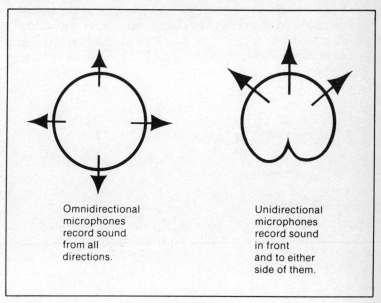

Omnidirectional
microphones
record sound
from all
directions.

Unidirectional
microphones
record sound
in front
and to either
side of them.

2. Condenser microphones

The second kind of microphone is the condenser mike. It is far more sensitive and cannot be handled roughly at all. It also needs a dry-cell battery to function. The condenser microphone is primarily used in the studio because it provides a wider frequency response than dynamic microphones.

3. Other microphones

Another type of microphone you will come across is the lapel microphone, also called a lavalier. It was invented for television and on-camera use where it was deemed visually crude to show a microphone. For the radio journalist, the lapel microphone is rarely practical because it often produces muddy sound. It is omnidirectional and too far away from the speaker's mouth to deliver good quality sound.

Some companies manufacture stereo microphones. One housing contains two recording capsules on a swivel, and they can be switched from 90°, to 120°, to 150°, to 180°, according to your needs. The cheap models are too noisy to produce good sound; better models require batteries, and still others need a heavy battery pack. (See chapter 8, Using a Microphone.)

d. PARAPHERNALIA

To record, edit, and listen to taped sound you need the following pieces of equipment.

1. Headphones

Headphones allow you to monitor the kind of sound your microphone picks up while you are recording sound or voice. Hence, you know what kind of signal the tape records. This is important for four reasons:

- You may have forgotten to switch a lever or press a button so what you believe is being recorded is not. That happens more often than you might think. By using headphones you will know what goes into the tape recorder.
- You can monitor the level of sound being recorded, any distortion of the signal from a sudden gust of wind, or any sudden boost in level.

You may have to re-record the interview or the sounds if the signal is distorted. Distorted sound cannot be equalized in the studio by even the most capable sound engineer.

- You can monitor ambient noise, such as traffic or overhead aircraft. The headphones will let you monitor exactly what the microphone picks up, so that you know when to stop recording and wait for the sound to pass, or to change your location. The headphones serve as notice of what not to record.
- You will know when your wrist movements or your wandering fingers on the microphone are producing crackling sounds that will spoil your recordings. Unless you are very experienced and know how to hold the mike rock steady, these sounds are likely.

What kind of headphones should you buy? There are two kinds that apply to your work, open-air headphones and the enclosed headset, which isolates your ears.

When you do an interview in a relatively quiet room, a simple pair of lightweight headphones will do. This type comes with the portable Walkman-type cassette recorders. They are called open-air headphones, cost very little, are padded with polyfoam, and are reasonably good.

The more expensive headphones fit over the entire ear and are used either in noisy environments or in a studio. They are heavier, but indispensable for the professional.

2. Sound mixer

A sound mixer combines soundtracks, in mono or stereo, on one tape. Mixers are used in the studio and rarely in the field because they are bulky and need an external power source. Unless you plan to run the entire show yourself, including mixing your product during the final taping, leave the mixing to a professional sound engineer (see chapter 16, The Final Montage).

3. Windsock

Microphones are sensitive to wind noise; a polyfoam cover, called a windsock, that fits over the microphone's recording head will eliminate most wind noise. Then you can monitor the level of sound using your headphone to listen for the odd gust of wind that will affect your recording regardless of the precautions you use.

Using a windsock will also prevent speakers' *p*'s from popping. If your subjects are popping their *p*'s, ask them to say: "Peter Piper picked a pickled pepper . . ." while you check whether the windsock has eliminated the popping sound (which, by the way, cannot be edited out later).

Unfortunately, windsocks will reduce the crispness of the sound recorded. (See Figure #3.)

4. Umbrella

I have found that always including a folding umbrella in my recording kit makes good sense. I use it while working in the field, because sudden rain could ruin my recording equipment.

But an umbrella has a second use. Should you have to record while a steady wind is blowing, and you discover that you are recording rumbling sounds despite using a windsock, open your umbrella and hold it just in front of the microphone to deflect the wind. The sound you intend to record will still filter through to your microphone. I once recorded the sounds of a stern-wheeler during strong winds by holding my umbrella in front of the microphone. The excessive wind noise would otherwise have made the recording unusable.

5. Shock absorber

Shock absorbers, or cradle suspensions, for microphones are essential. They eliminate most of the sounds generated when you move microphones around while you record. The main component of shock absorbers is two stiff rubber flanges that do not conduct sound; the microphone clips into them. (See Figures #4 and #5.)

6. Pistol grip

A pistol grip lets you hold your microphone for a long period without tiring. It is made of hard rubber or wood,

FIGURE #3
MICROPHONE WINDSOCK

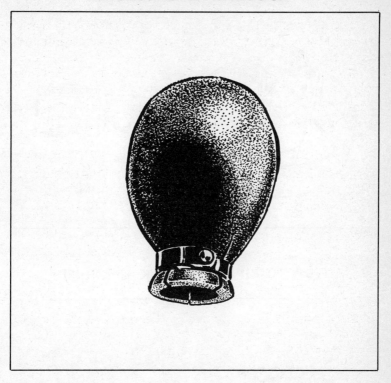

and it screws into the microphone holder (or the shock absorber) so you can carry the microphone comfortably and without tiring your fingers. (See Figure #5.)

7. T-bar

A T-bar is used to record in stereo in the field. It is a piece of metal, either rigid or foldable, with screws on either end, to which you mount two microphones in an XY or AB configuration (see chapter 8, Using a Microphone). The pistol grip then attaches underneath the T-bar so you can carry the stereo rig in comfort. (See Figure #6.)

FIGURE #4
CRADLE SUSPENSION

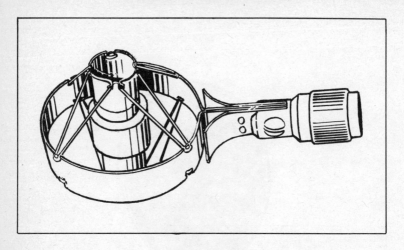

FIGURE #5
PISTOL GRIP AND SHOCK ABSORBER

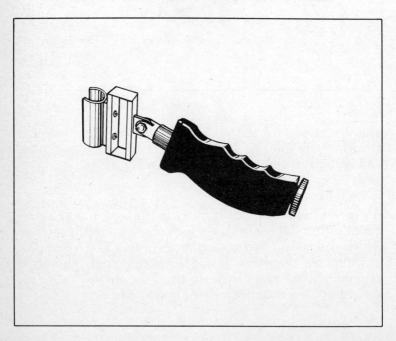

FIGURE #6
T-BAR

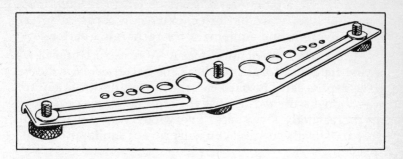

8. Cords and connectors

Most microphones are not sold with cords, so you will have to make them up to fit your microphone. Get a good, sturdy microphone cord and ask to have state-of-the-art metal connectors installed. Avoid connectors with plastic housing because cords often trail on the ground and a plastic connector will crack if it is stepped on. By the same token, the cord should be relatively thick so it cannot twist and break under stress.

Coiled microphone cord is not a good idea as it tends to tangle up. While working in the field, you have enough cords to worry about.

9. Editing block

Editing blocks are made of either aluminum or plastic. Get the heaviest type made from metal, preferably one that has the 90°, 60°, and 45° slots. The dovetail groove in an editing block is precision-machined to a tolerance slightly narrower than the width of quarter-inch tape. The tape must be pressed firmly but gently into this groove, which holds the tape in place while you mark it, cut it with the razor blade, and splice it with splicing tape. (See Figure #7 and chapter 12, How to Pick, Save, and Discard.)

10. Other equipment

Other equipment is essential to your recording kit. Always carry leader tape, splicing tape, grease pencils, razor blades, head cleaning fluid, and a recording head demagnetizer. As well, include in your kit small precision screwdrivers, labels, a pencil, a penknife, scissors, patchcords, duct tape, masking tape, spare batteries, extension cords, adapters for connectors, and equipment for recharging batteries.

An acquaintance of mine once went to record interviews in the field and forgot to check his batteries. Nor did he have a spare set. The batteries ran down, the documentary was almost scotched because the tape had been recorded at an increasingly slow pace. Everybody was unhappy. Be prepared in all ways and you will prevent similar problems.

FIGURE #7
EDITING BLOCK AND RAZOR BLADE

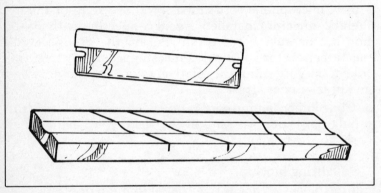

Do not let this extensive list of hardware and auxiliary equipment intimidate you. You can equip yourself to the standard of most radio productions for a few hundred dollars if you buy only what you need. But you must also buy wisely. A secondhand state-of-the-art portable cassette recorder (with at least a 90-day repair warranty) is often a better choice than a new second-rate machine that costs the same.

Before you buy anything, seek the advice of an experienced radio journalist, then double-check everything with a good sound engineer. Most professionals will not hesitate to give free advice.

8

USING A MICROPHONE

A microphone transmits sound to the magnetic track on a length of recording tape via electrical signal. If that signal is poor because your microphone is of inferior construction, your radio documentary will suffer. Likewise, if you move the microphone erratically during recording, or don't record properly in other ways, the tape you produce will be unusable.

Therefore, choose the best microphone you can afford (see chapter 7, section c.) Then, take the time to read the instruction manual that comes with it. Every microphone has different characteristics, and unless you know them and acknowledge their peculiarities, you may not achieve your microphone's best performance.

As well, follow the recommendations in this chapter to make usable and satisfactory recordings.

a. HAND-HELD VERSUS MOUNTED MICROPHONES

There are two schools of thought concerning where you should position your microphone while recording an interview. One school says you should hold the microphone in your hand, while the other says you should first mount it on a tripod, then put it on a firm base.

1. Using a hand-held microphone

A hand-held microphone offers a great deal of flexibility because it allows you to adjust the distance between microphone and speaker, which is important to recording quality.

But if you use a hand-held microphone, never point it directly at your interviewee. That can be construed as a distressingly aggressive act.

Instead, hold your microphone vertically, a foot away and six inches below the interviewee's mouth. This position works well for both omnidirectional and unidirectional microphones.

Use a shock absorber, or cradle suspension, to reduce handling noise; also consider using a pistol grip. (See chapter 7, section d.). As well, some news reporters loop the microphone cord around their fist while holding the microphone in their hand. This prevents the cord from generating cord noise. The more sensitive a microphone, the more safeguards it needs from handling noise.

Above all, remember to hold your hand rock steady while hand-holding your microphone. Any twisting movement will generate sound, although lateral movements while holding your wrist still will not. Your headphones will tell you whether you have created any handling noise.

2. Using a mounted microphone

Mounting a microphone on a tripod, then setting it on a firm surface is one of the safest ways of avoiding handling noise. But even here there are hidden dangers.

First, a tripod-mounted mike is in a fixed position and cannot follow the speaker's involuntary body movements. Hence the sound often drifts to low levels. To solve this problem, you could adjust the volume level on your recorder, which results in higher background noise, you could use a hand-held mike that follows the speaker's movements, or alternatively, you could use a wire neck mount. This is a contraption fashioned from heavy-gauge steel wire that loops around the speaker's neck. At the end is a clamp that holds the microphone firmly in place.

Second, you have to swivel a mounted mike on its tripod to record your voice. To avoid the resulting handling noise, use two microphones and record on different tracks. Unfortunately, this solution also doubles the ambient noise, so it only works when you are recording in a sound-proof room.

b. STEREO RIGS

To rig a stereo recording system, mount two similar microphones, preferably of the same make and type, at opposite corners of a T-bar. There are two basic configurations.

1. AB stereo mode

In the AB stereo mode, the microphones are mounted parallel to each other. This mode is normally used only for recording orchestras or choirs (see Figure #8).

The distance between the two recording heads is important. If the microphones are closer to the sound source than three times their distance apart, you will have phasing problems. These affect the mono compatibility of stereo sound and make the recording faint, distant, and somewhat tinny. Phasing problems render a recording practically worthless.

2. XY stereo mode

In the XY stereo mode, the microphone heads either point away from each other or point toward one another at a 90° to 120° angle (see Figure #9).

Be careful how you identify the two cords leading from your microphones to the recorder. You could color-code the cords.

3. Technique

With a stereo rig the advantages of using hand-held versus mounted microphones are reversed. A hand-held rig is more difficult to control than a mounted rig. It is generally heavy and, because you use only one hand on a stereo rig (you will need the other to scratch your nose, to adjust your headphones, and, mostly, to twiddle knobs and flip switches on your portable recorder), your arm can tire to

FIGURE #8
AB STEREO CONFIGURATION

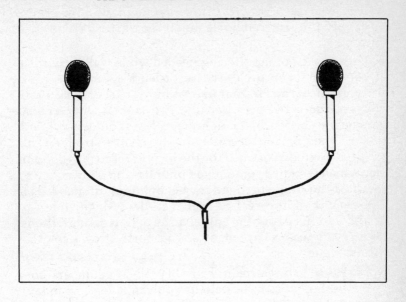

FIGURE #9
XY STEREO CONFIGURATION

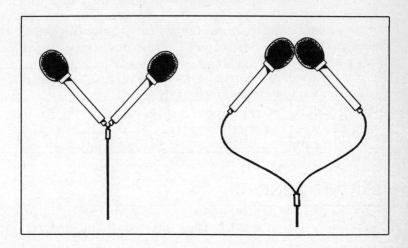

the point of trembling. To avoid the handling noise such trembling would generate, and to support your arm so it doesn't weaken when you move, try to move your entire body with the arm that holds the stereo rig; hold your wrist still.

The amount of monitoring needed while walking with a stereo rig is even greater. I recorded a 15-minute walk through the Grand Bazaar in Istanbul as part of my Orient Express radio feature. Luckily, the friend who accompanied me carried his daughter on his shoulders while I pushed the portable recorder in the child's stroller. The stroller created a cosy bed for the heavy stereo microphone rig (which weighed some seven pounds) and allowed me to monitor the sound through my headphones unimpeded by the weight of the reel-to-reel recorder. Meanwhile my friend and his daughter enjoyed the action around them. The result was an excellent sound portrait of a colorful ethnic scene.

Carrying a stereo rig in the field is always cumbersome. Get a backup person to help, if you can, even if it means hiring someone off the street.

c. CORDS AND CONNECTORS

All sound recording equipment is fragile, including the cords that connect the mike to the recorder. They should not be twisted, knotted, or stepped on. The cord's most fragile part is where it is soldered to the connectors. If you pull a cord out of a socket, remember to grasp the connector, not the cord, or eventually it will break loose and cause a bad connection when you use it to record.

You are at the mercy of your location while in the field. Carry a spare set of microphone cords with connectors in your kit bag and you will always be on top of the situation.

d. MONITORING

There is a distinct psychological aspect to wearing a pair of headphones that cut out extraneous sound and register only what the microphones pick up. It's like entering another acoustic dimension because it distorts reality. Until you have worn headphones and carried a stereo rig, you won't know what a strange and wonderful surprise is in store for you.

The first time you wear headphones and carry a stereo rig, go to a tennis court and close your eyes as you listen to the ball bounce back and forth. When you open your eyes, you will start looking beside you and behind you because the sound seems to come from everywhere at once. You would think 12 tennis games were going on instead of one. It is a weird sensation. Once you adjust to wearing headphones, you will find them invaluable for monitoring your recordings. As well, they can tell you when your microphone picks up an extraneous sound.

Monitoring your recordings will keep you busy. Although you will be interviewing and having to digest what is said as well as prepare your next question, at the same time, you must watch the volume unit (VU) meter so you can adjust the recording level; you must listen for distortions and for unwanted background noise; and you must watch to see the tape is rolling. (Some people depress the "pause" button and forget to release it, which means they can hear the words going into the recorder but nothing is being recorded because the cassette has been stopped.) It takes practice before the technique is mastered.

1. Recording level

The recording level on your recorder (usually on a scale of one to ten) should be around the eight mark for most microphones. For condenser mikes, it might be around six or seven.

Throughout the recording session, watch the VU meter. On older tape recorders it will have clock-like hands. Light-emitting diode (LED) meters come with the newer tape recorders. Their electronic response time is more instant than the mechanical hands of the VU meters, but they are impossible to read in bright light.

The needle on the VU meter (or the LED lights) should peak just past the zero mark and swing a little into the "+" field, no more than two to three decibels (dBs). If the gain is set too high the sound will distort; if it is too low you will hear an unpleasant hiss. Follow the recommendations in the tape recorder instruction manual. (See Figure #10.)

FIGURE #10
VOLUME UNIT METER

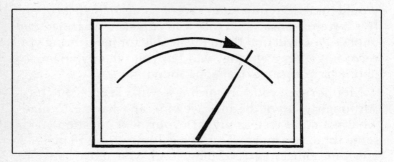

2. Generated noise

The VU meter needle will jump or the LED lights will flash when your microphone picks up generated noise. You are monitoring to catch such increases, so watch and listen for them.

Generated noise is both external and internal. It can be noise on the street, in a building, or in nature, as well as noise generated by loose cords, rough handling of the mike, or similar mishaps.

Your interviewees may generate a lot of noise and make life hard for you. They may pick up the cord and twiddle with it, they may tap or bang on the table, or they may move the tripod around while talking. All these movements generate handling noise that cannot be removed later in the studio. If your interviewees start fiddling, stop recording and politely explain why you want them to cease and desist. Nobody will mind such a request, and it will save you much frustration with generated noise later.

Also, avoid locations that are targets for unwanted sound, even if the source is hundreds of yards away. Sound travels upward more than downward, a fact that might influence your choice of locations.

Unless your project calls for specific background noise, try to avoid anything that registers through your headphones. Listen before you record; take your time; re-record if necessary. Generated noise is one of the worst enemies of the sound recordist.

3. Ambient noise

Ambient noise is much more friendly and often quite pleasant. In nature you can hear ambient noise that might provide a good backdrop for a radio project. It is best, though, to record ambient noise separately and conduct any interviews in an enclosed room or a more soundproof environment. Voice and ambient noise can be mixed later.

Sometimes ambient noises combine to make recording conditions perfect. I once recorded a Doukhobor funeral. Realizing the Doukhobors are known for their a cappella singing, I wanted to record the choir. As it sang a number of hymns, the gravediggers lowered the casket into the ground and started shovelling the earth, which fell on the casket in clumps. I held the stereo rig by hand, positioning myself so that the powerful choir was 50 feet away and the gravediggers 20 feet away. The result was one of the most moving recordings that conveyed what happens at a funeral and interment ceremony. Its beauty was achieved by a combination of generated and ambient noise at its best.

Ambient noise is usually soft and used to develop atmosphere. Record as much as you can whenever you can. As you build up your sound library, you will be able to use these sounds over and over again for new productions. (See chapter 9, Recording Sound Effects and Music.)

4. Hums

A hum is a low-level noise, often generated by electronic equipment or by interference. Some cheaper tape and cassette recorders have been known to create hums. Faulty soldering on cords to connectors can create them too, as can overhead neon lights, power stations, and nearby machinery.

A hum is difficult to remove later, and sometimes it cannot be filtered out in the studio. If you are not sure whether you have a hum, record something, then go to a quiet place and play it back. Change locations if you hear a hum.

e. SOME RECORDING TIPS

• Learn to pause between an answer and your next question; it will make editing your tape much easier.

• Record some room noise after the interview by holding up your free hand and asking for silence. Room noise is needed for adding pauses in tight spots while editing.

• If someone is giving a speech that is being magnified over a public address system, tape your microphone to the mike stand (remember to carry duct or masking tape). This way you will record the speaker directly, rather than through the loudspeakers, which always distort and produce poor results.

9

RECORDING SOUND EFFECTS AND MUSIC

Sound effects are called "SFX" in the broadcasting vernacular. They are sounds that occur naturally, or they are generated artificially, in a range from the soft and lyrical to the strident and powerful.

SFX have come to occupy their own place in radio. The pioneers of radio drama probably used SFX; a sound effects technician would create the sounds of doors opening, telephones ringing, people walking, and horses galloping. These were mono SFX and rather primitive. But they achieved their purpose to create a mood, heighten a dramatic moment, or provide transition to the next scene.

With the advent of stereophonic sound, the perfection of portable recording equipment and the introduction of Dolby noise reduction technology, SFX engineers became more adventurous and started collecting and storing sounds they recorded in the field as well as those recorded in the studio.

The international radio features produced in the seventies and eighties made extensive use of superbly recorded SFX; in fact, Peter Leonhard Braun's classic radio feature, "The Bells of Europe," produced in West Berlin, elevated SFX to star status.

Then, in 1979, Hollywood film director Francis Ford Coppola used SFX combined with powerful music in his film, *Apocalypse Now*. In that film a squadron of gunships attack to the beat of helicopter blades, the roar of engine exhausts, and the strains of a Wagner opera blasting from loudspeakers in the leading gunship. SFX and high-decibel music unite as a psychological weapon against the enemy and a dramatic entertainment for the audience.

The radio documentarist can use SFX to equal, if not greater, advantage. With a mixture of sound effects, a documentarist can create a sound image — an assembly of acoustic associations — that the listener immediately identifies.

Recorded music can also be used to enhance a radio documentary: sometimes to dramatize a passage, sometimes to serve as background, or as transition between two segments. You can use commercially recorded or "canned" music, or record your own music in the field. Either way, you may encounter legal problems unless the music is in the public domain and, therefore, can be used without permission and at no cost. If the composer holds copyright, you must gain permission and pay royalties.

A general caution: When you want to record SFX in the field, be aware that not everyone may want to be recorded. Use the same courteous approach you would use when trying to photograph a shoeshine boy or market vendor in Mexico, for example. Ask permission first and, if necessary, negotiate a fee. If you don't, you might run into well-deserved trouble.

Recording people without their consent is an invasion of privacy, perhaps not always in the legal sense (depending on the circumstances) but certainly in the ethical sense. The boundaries between good taste and offensive behavior are not always clearly defined. Remember that not all media people are revered and respected, especially not in Third World countries.

a. NATURAL SOUND EFFECTS

You might be tempted to think that all natural sound effects are straightforward. But every microphone distorts reality, no matter how good it is. The SFX a microphone records often do not sound identical to the way your ear hears the sound at its source. Any good SFX engineer can play you sounds you won't be able to identify correctly. But that doesn't really matter. You use sound as dramatis personae, as the carriers of an acoustic message in your production.

Each natural sound has its own personality. Some sounds set certain moods; for example, the foreboding of dogs barking at a distance, the anxiety of howling wind and crashing thunder, or the impatience of horses stomping and neighing. Some sounds set the scene; for example, the seaside with a seagull's cry, the farm with a cow chewing her cud, or a mountain cave with the echo of slowly dripping water. And some sounds set the time of day; for example, morning birdsong.

But natural sounds — just because they depict life in a barn, in a meadow, beside a brook, on the range, or in a corral — are often difficult to record because they are too near civilization with all its mechanical noise. You may have to travel a fair distance to get away from the unwanted, but persistent, noise of the city and highway. And of course, when you do find a quiet place, just as you are about to capture the buzzing of bees and hornets, an airplane will fly overhead and spoil your recording. Therefore, to record certain sound effects in nature you need the patience of Job.

The array of natural sounds you may want to record is virtually limitless. Among the most satisfying activities in broadcasting are developing the art of capturing these diverse sounds, perfecting your technique, using the best equipment, and building your archive of SFX. You will be in tune with life at its source.

b. GENERATED SOUND EFFECTS

Generated sound effects are sounds that occur more frequently in a high-tech society. They are certainly the most pervasive and intrusive of all sounds. Explosions, gun and cannon fire, blaring radio and TV sets, and thousands of different mechanical devices and clattering machines are all part of our acoustic environment 24 hours a day.

Many of these human- and machine-generated noises are offensive and constitute a health hazard because their decibel value exceeds safe levels. There would be no sense in using traffic noise as a sound effect in most cases — the sound is too abrasive.

There are, however, generated sounds that lend themselves well for use in documentaries and features. Crowd noise, sawing, chopping wood, someone crying, a child babbling, a person humming, a fog horn, a ship's whistle, boats creaking at a wooden dock, the hammering in a blacksmith's shop, the distinctive sounds of machinery in factories or shops — all can be used effectively.

Whenever you can, record any generated sounds you think might be useful. Sooner or later you will be able to use them for accent, transition, background, ambiance, mood, or as leading components in your production.

c. MUSIC

The variety of usable music available outside the protection of composers' or performers' copyright is wide enough that you can avoid paying royalties or fees. Here is a short list of the type of music available:

- Folk songs performed by amateurs who have consented to being recorded
- Marching brass bands who perform on holidays or during parades
- Organ music at a wedding or a funeral
- Choirs singing or orchestras playing in a public place; for example, the orchestras that play in the cafes on the Piazza San Marco in Venice (These are recorded strictly from a distance and intended merely to set the acoustic scene in your production.)

If you intend to use this music solely to accentuate your program, you will rarely get into difficulty, simply because the recorded music extract is not long enough to constitute a complete composition and has not been recorded to acoustical perfection, which means it could not be used to produce commercial music recordings for sale.

One important criterion about the legality of using a music extract that you have recorded in your documentary or feature should be that it cannot stand on its own but is part of a montage. If you have any qualms about what is proper, get advice from your producer or the radio station's contract lawyer.

In all cases it makes good sense not to offend the unwritten rules of ethical behavior, just as obeying legal restrictions should be part of your professional attitude. On the subject of music copyright and its infringement, refer to the *Musician's Handbook*, another title in the Self-Counsel Series.

d. HOW TO RECORD SOUND EFFECTS AND MUSIC

You must stalk natural sound effects as you would stalk a bird with your camera. Record what you can with your stereo rig, but you may have to sacrifice stereo for mono when the sounds are too far away. Then, use a shotgun microphone to bridge the distance between you and the sound source, or consider using a parabolic microphone that spans even greater distances, at the expense of fidelity.

Because their range is so great, shotgun and parabolic microphones can only pinpoint and record a narrow slice of sound in the distance, and the result is a mono recording. For a stereo recording to create the illusion of a full 180° spectrum, each microphone needs a 90° range, which is typical of unidirectional microphones. The shotgun or parabolic microphone often covers a spectrum of no more than 10°. However, in combination with other sounds, voices, and music in a studio production, your mono sound will make a valuable contribution to the end product.

High frequency sounds, such as trickling water and birdsong overload the recording at a lower VU level than, for instance, the human voice. When recording one of these natural SFX, remember to keep the recording level lower than you think is proper and the VU meter appears to indicate.

e. MORE SUGGESTIONS FOR RECORDING IN THE FIELD

1. Handling your recorder

To carry your cassette recorder, keep the shoulder strap very short so you can hang the recorder around your neck and low on your chest (just above your waist) where you can look down at the controls. You'll see some field recordists carrying their recorders over their shoulders. But this is inconvenient when you want to watch the VU meter or the LED readout scale; you'll have to twist your head during the recording, which makes for a sore neck and missed action. While carrying your recorder around your neck may not look as stylish as dangling it from your shoulder, remember that your object is not to impress but to bring home good sound.

Another reason for carrying your recorder around your neck is that when you walk or run to catch a disappearing sound source, it will stay in place. If you carry it over your shoulder, it will likely slide off.

If you want to be really up-to-date, get yourself a Cuban hitch, a contraption available at camera stores. This hitch is just the right size to strap your portable cassette recorder firmly to your chest so you can move at speed without worrying about it bouncing or sliding.

2. Handling other equipment

You will most likely want to bring along a kit bag for all your other recording paraphernalia. Don't — it will just get in the way.

You can put your windsocks, spare batteries, folded umbrella, spare cassettes in the voluminous pockets of a windbreaker or parka, or in your pants, which should be baggy and have inside and outside pockets. You cannot have too many pockets when recording in the field.

You will also want to fill your pockets with your money, your ID, and your official pass or letter of introduction if you have one.

3. Fades

When you begin recording sounds or music in the field, set the recording volume control knob at zero and start the tape. Then monitor through your headphones, and as the sound gradually emerges, slowly turn up the control knob until both your headphones and your meter tell you the recording level is perfect. Stop there, but keep adjusting the control knob because sounds and music in the field have a tendency to change in volume.

This operation is called fading in the sound. When you have recorded enough, don't just hit the stop button, but slowly turn the recording volume control knob back to zero. That's called fading out the sound.

The purpose of fading is that, later on, when you assemble your components, you may need a ready-made sound or music sequence that can be spliced into the master tape. If the sound or the music is fairly constant and won't walk away from you, record a series of short segments with fade-ins and fade-outs at 5, 7, 10, 15, 20, or 30 seconds, whatever length segment you think may be useful later on. A distinct segment is then available to be dubbed because you remembered to fade your SFX and music recording in and out while in the field. Although a sound engineer can do all this in the studio, you save time, effort, and script stages by having SFX or music segments of various lengths ready to be edited in.

I learned the value of fading by trial and error over many years of field practice. Following these recommendations is a shortcut to professional recording practices.

f. SUMMING UP

Sound effects will take much of your time should you decide to record them yourself in the field. Many radio stations have archives of sound effects; SFX are also available on commercial records. Certainly music has never been offered in greater variety or quality than today. You may, therefore, wish to go that route, gaining permission from the artist and paying royalties.

If, however, you want to be in control of all aspects of a sound production, you have the time, you have dealt with all potential legal hassles, and you have the necessary high-quality equipment, then go forth and record.

10

DUBBING RECORDED MATERIAL

Dubbing refers to the process of copying a signal from one tape recorder to another, just as files are copied between computers or from disc to disc.

All you need is two tape recorders: the source, or originating recorder, and the destination, or receiving recorder. The originating recorder is usually a portable cassette recorder, a cassette deck or a portable reel-to-reel tape recorder; the destination recorder is almost always a studio-sized or table-top reel-to-reel (quarter-inch) tape recorder.

As you know by now, the state-of-the-art portable cassette recorders are good enough, and deliver broadcast quality sound, to be used on remote locations or in the field. Take advantage of this high mobility. Also take advantage of the low cost of cassette tapes (but use reputable manufacturers of cassette tape only). Then you will always have first-class original recordings from which you can make any number of quarter-inch tape dubs for editing.

Another advantage to using cassettes for original recordings is that you always have a complete, uncut recording because you keep the originals and edit the dubs.

If you carefully follow every step that is discussed below, you will come up with near perfect copies, or dubs. Please remember, however, that your original tape is the first generation. Any dub you make is the second generation and will lose some sharpness and fidelity. A dub of a dub will be third generation, with an even less sharply defined signal, and so on down the line. Most sound productions wind up with fifth and sixth generation dubs. The better the original signal is, the better chance you have of getting a good end product.

With the advent of digital sound, the problem of diminishing quality has been eliminated. The portable, affordable digital recorders are still to be introduced to the consumer market.

a. PATCH CORDS

When dubbing tapes, your first need is for a patch cord that connects your line out on the originating recorder to the line in on the receiving recorder. There are several kinds of connectors between recorders: the XLR connectors; the European Phillips plugs; the so-called telephone plugs; the RCA plugs; and the mini-plugs. For most applications, you will need RCA plugs, but sometimes you need an adapter or a patch cord with two different plugs.

Keep all the patch cords that come with the hardware you buy over the years. You never know when you might need an extra one. You may also get a variety of adapter plugs and keep them in reserve.

b. SETTINGS

The originating recorder must be set for the kind of tape you used for the original recording. Type I (normal) or Type II (chrome-dioxide) are the most common kinds of tape. Few people use Type III (ferrochromium) or IV (metal-dioxide) cassette tape anymore. Recent quality advances in Type II tape have made Types III and IV virtually superfluous. Most cassette decks and portables do very well with Types I and II. Check twice that you have adjusted the tape setting to the kind of tape originally used before dubbing.

Next, adjust the Dolby noise reduction button. If you have recorded with Dolby B or C, the originating recorder should be adjusted to the corresponding setting. If you forget to set the Dolby adjustment, you will forfeit the benefits of Dolby and transmit a signal with a lot of tape hiss to your dubbed tape.

The volume level on the originating recorder does not affect the recording level on the receiving recorder. You can ignore it.

Now look at the receiving recorder. Most reel-to-reels won't have a Dolby system, so you can ignore that aspect. But they may have a bewildering array of settings, including the following —

- AUX for auxiliary
- LINE IN/LINE OUT
- MIC I and II for microphone one and two
- REC for record
- PLAY for playback
- PLAY/REC for playback/record
- PAUSE
- TUNER
- PHONO for the turntable

The best way to learn what all these terms mean is to read the instruction manual that comes with your recorder.

Set the recording speed to the same speed you used when recording the tape. If the original tape was recorded at seven and a half inches per second, dub it at that speed, or the fidelity will suffer.

Once the originating and the receiving tape recorders have been connected using the proper patch cord, and all the knobs and buttons are in their correct settings, you need to connect your headphones to the receiving recorder so you can hear what's coming in. Finally, do a test run.

c. TEST RUN

Push the start button on the originating recorder. Unless you have an older model, the VU meter or the LED light should read that there is a signal going out. Older models only react to incoming, or recording, signals.

Then, push both the record and play buttons on the receiving recorder while simultaneously engaging the pause button. This activates the recording mode but stops the tape from rolling. Then your headphones will register the incoming signal level.

Next, adjust the volume knob until the peaks of the incoming signal just swoop past the O-VU (zero) calibration. Check that it sounds good and that there is no distortion. Try to find the loudest incoming signal and keep your volume level knob there.

Professionals use a tone generator to put a one kHz tone at the beginning of a tape, then they calibrate the receiving recorder precisely. Tone generators are available at a reasonable price, but unless you do a lot of tricky dubbing, you can save yourself the money. On the other hand, it will make your sound engineer much happier if you record a one kHz tone on your tape.

When all the settings look right, shut everything down, and make a few last minute checks before dubbing.

d. DUBBING

Before you begin, use this checklist to double-check everything:

- Have you wound back the originating cassette tape to the zero mark?
- Does the receiving recorder have the same amount of blank tape available as the originating cassette tape will transmit?
- Have you demagnetized the recording, playback, and erasing heads of both recorders recently?
- Have you cleaned the heads of both recorders? (This is not an idle reminder. I once sold an older model cassette recorder to a friend who complained, half a year later, that it was a bum recorder because it chewed up cassettes. When I asked him if he had ever cleaned the heads, he admitted he hadn't. After a thorough cleaning there was no longer any problem.

Now you are ready to start dubbing. Push the start and record buttons of the receiving recorder simultaneously;

then engage the pause button again. This practice ensures that the machine will be up to speed as soon as you disengage the pause button. Double-check that you have disengaged the pause button.

Start the originating recorder and monitor the incoming sound through your headphones. Is the signal strong and up to speed? Is there no distortion? Then let the two recorders do their transmitting and receiving while you monitor the action through your headphones from time to time.

When everything has been dubbed, roll back the tape on the receiving recorder a few feet and listen, just to double-check the signal is there. This is unnecessary if you are using a three-head tape recorder, which will allow you to monitor the sound you have just recorded.

e. LEVELS

While learning to make recordings, you may not always record at the same level. Some levels will be high, some low. These recordings need to be equalized and adjusted. As a rule, this is the kind of work studio engineers do.

The advantage of dubbing is that the test run of recording levels will virtually assure the dubbed tape has a balanced signal. Any high or low levels in your original recording can be leveled off while you dub, monitoring constantly, and adjusting the recording level on the receiving recorder as needed.

You may prefer to dub your tapes yourself unless you can be sure that the studio engineer is well qualified and dependable. When someone else dubs your cassettes there is a possibility that the dubbing will not be monitored properly and that mistakes will be made. That means you may have to work with a dub that has flaws.

In my experience the only person that can be trusted completely is the documentarist. People who are not directly involved in a project often have scant interest in the product. Their attention may wander, and dubs can be lost or marred. Further, sometimes the original cassette can be lost, or misplaced, or erased accidentally. The most improbable mishaps can occur when you give tapes to others to be dubbed.

f. SUMMING UP

Dubbing tape from one recorder to another is professional work that requires a high level of concentration. If you forget to flip one lever, or forget to turn one knob, you will have an inferior tape copy or perhaps no dub at all.

Maintain your equipment and treat everything with as much care as you give raw eggs, and you will avoid most problems and develop good dubbing technique.

11

REVIEWING YOUR COMPONENTS

In chapter 4 you learned how to get organized by defining
your project, determining the approach, making a flow
chart, setting a schedule, establishing a work pattern, and
checking the overview.

If you have followed these recommendations, done the
research, recorded the interviews, assembled the SFX and
music, it is time to get reorganized and to review all your
components before their assembly can begin.

A review of all your components at this stage will save
you from scrambling to find one last piece when your time
is up.

a. BACKGROUND

Now that you have gathered all the components, ready for
further processing, take another look at the background of
the story you are about to tell. Is the central idea still valid
several weeks or months later? Is the story's angle holding
up now that you have investigated all aspects of the story?
Does it need to be refocused or even discarded for a new
story?

The background is what makes a story in a documentary
or feature feasible. It is its context in relation to society, to
politics, to economics, and to culture. Knowing a story's
background means you understand why certain people
behave in a certain way in a certain situation. Being aware
of a story's background gives you the needed edge.

b. INTERVIEWS

By now, all your interviews have been recorded and
dubbed, and the original tapes sit in labeled boxes. Review

the people interviewed by consulting your notes. Have they all told you as much as you need from them? If not, should you try to interview someone else to fill the gap before you start final assembly? Do it now while you're still ahead; it won't take too much time or throw your schedule awry.

c. TRANSITIONS

Transitions are used in any story — radio, print, or television. Sometimes a story comes to a dead stop after you have finished exploring an angle. To get back into the main body of your story you need a transition.

At its crudest, a transition in radio is an unrelated piece of music or a pleasant but meaningless SFX sequence. At its best, a transition is smooth and elegant, and converts a cul de sac into a thoroughfare. Transitions resemble the splicing tape with which you join two edited lengths of audio tape — two pieces become one again.

The most common transition is a written piece of narration. You inform the listener who has just spoken, who is next, and you provide a link between two ideas to carry the story forward.

But also use SFX and music for transition. Listeners may need a few seconds to digest what you present, especially when they have just heard you develop a major thought.

In conversation, you would give your listener silence; but silence is regarded as a deadly sin of omission in radio broadcasting. Silence means that the listener might change stations. Or, if someone has just tuned in and they hear nothing they will change stations again. Instead of silence put in a sound sequence or a piece of music, ideally something that reflects the mood of the thought just developed.

At this point in your production, it is too early to worry about specifics. Review your transitions simply to ensure that you have enough material for transitions when you are ready. If you don't have enough, perhaps you have an overflow from all the SFX and music selections you have collected. Otherwise, get extra SFX and music segments now while you still have time on your hands.

d. SOUND EFFECTS

Review all the sound effects you have recorded or acquired. If you aren't sure what you have, listen to all your tapes and make a detailed list of each one, with the time each SFX segment runs. Does the sound effect fade in smoothly? Does it fade out so you can use it as an entire sequence? Are all the SFX in stereo, or are some in mono? You may have to re-record some of them now at your leisure. Make a note of these particulars.

e. MUSIC

Music provides different worrying aspects. Unless you have recorded folk or other music in the field, and are planning to use that to illustrate or embroider your feature, you may want to use commercially recorded music on LPs, compact discs, or cassettes.

The cost of buying recorded music just for your production can be high. Of course, you may claim legitimate expenses on your income tax return, but you still need the cash up front. If you have access to a record library, you are doing well. A record library either at the radio station or at public or university libraries reduces the cost, but it takes time to sift through all the titles to find what you need.

Part of the job of finding the right kind of music is to talk to people who know more about music than you do. Draw them into your project, and explain the mood and the background of the scene you want to illustrate with music. They might be able to help steer you in the right direction.

I once needed theme music for a four-part series of features, each one an hour long. The music had to be heavy and menacing, indicating disaster and oppression, which was the theme of the feature. The record librarian suggested an opera by a contemporary Polish composer, based on the historic case of a witch hunt. It took only ten minutes to find the passage which was to introduce the four-part series and scare the listeners out of their wits. Without the librarian's help, I would never have found such a descriptive piece of music.

Once you have assessed what music is available, check that you have permissions, catalog everything, time it, and make sure the LPs are in good shape, without scratches, repeats, or flaws. (There are ways to repair some of the damage to records. Good sound engineers, using sophisticated equipment, can filter most of the faults out and dub music from record to tape, which will guarantee that you have music that can be used when needed.)

f. QUOTATIONS

A radio script needs quotes to round out the flow of the program. Quotes are not always necessary, but they have their place, especially when read well by a professional.

Use a dictionary of quotations to find some that are suitable for your program. Other sources are books, magazines, periodicals, journals, dissertations, position papers, letters, advertisements, flyers, labels or any other printed matter connected with your topic. Your basic research at the beginning of your project will have given you access to a number of good passages to be used for the script.

Don't worry if you end up with so much material you don't know what to do with it. Throwing stuff away later is always better than having to research when you are on deadline.

Organize all your quotes; type them neatly on separate sheets of paper, number them, and make an index so you can find them again. Then put them away for later reference.

g. READERS

At this time, you and your producer should look around for a reader for your quotations, who can "lift the words off a page," a reader who sounds natural, as if he or she is telling a story. A good reader is hard to find.

The secrets of "lifting the words off a page" are good cadence, rhythm, diction, pacing, accent, inflection, and articulation, plus lots of practice. These skills have to be learned.

If you have a budget that allows you to hire a professional reader, use it. Audition readers and have them stand by, making sure they are available when assembly time comes around. If you want them, but they are not available later on, ask them to record your quotes — even the extra ones — since readers are usually paid according to the length of the program, not the time it takes to read the material.

h. NARRATOR

A narrator can be either the author of the project, a station announcer (who comes free), or an actor.

If your delivery is good or could be improved, do it yourself. You will save time and money, and you can improve your script up to the last moment. If not, use an announcer. But many of them have voices too plummy for your purposes. They sound fairly good when they read the news in a grave voice with deep concern, they can sound like excited barkers when they do commercials, and sometimes they can even produce reasonable readings of a script — but not often.

For top quality, your best bet is to hire a professional.

i. SCRIPT

At this stage, your script is still in your mind but you have an approximate idea of how you will approach the subject.

The best scripts sound as if the reader is extemporizing. Therefore, a good script is not the same as a good magazine article. Writing for speech is different. The script must be short; the language must be simple; and the statements should be short and direct. (For more details about script, see chapter 15.)

j. SCHEDULE

Your schedule is determined by your deadline. Throughout your project you will have established, changed, discarded, and created yet another set of deadlines. The fewer times you do this the better, obviously. No one likes to work with a mercurial writer who cannot meet deadlines.

Why is it so important to follow a schedule? One reason is economic survival. Unless you set yourself a pace you can follow, you will waste so much time you won't be able to make a living. Second, unless you know what's coming up next, you are operating by guesswork, and that won't do.

Set your goals one by one following the sequence in this book. If need be, push yourself to finish in time. Adhering to a realistic set of deadlines is not creating a stressful working climate; quite the reverse. Working at speed and with vigor is immensely satisfying.

k. STUDIO TIME

Depending on what your circumstances are, and for whom you are producing your masterpiece, you might book studio time weeks ahead. Studios are always hard to book, especially those that specialize in recording rock music. Sound engineers are often booked separately.

Early booking will not only assure you of a studio when you need one, and of the engineer's time, but it will give you that ultimate deadline which you must not miss.

12

HOW TO PICK, SAVE, AND DISCARD

All your interview and sound effects recordings are, at this point, a mountain of recorded tape. Before you can edit them (as described in detail in chapter 13), you must pick what you want, save what you will use, and discard what you won't need. This process of choosing, saving, and eliminating is your first major test.

As you begin, ignore the recorded sound effects. They can keep until all the words have been dealt with. You want to be as sure as you can that you will choose the most important statements, put on hold those you aren't sure about, and put on an outs reel those you feel won't stand up. (If you keep an outs reel, you have the option of retrieval; always keep the backdoor open.)

The following list of steps is not sequential. For everything to function in this most decisive procedure of making judgments, of choosing, of saving, of bypassing, of discarding, of labeling, of keeping time, and of writing a synopsized transcript, you will be jumping back and forth between all these little jobs.

Warning: Don't be discouraged by the mass of things to do and remember. It all makes sense, it will all come together, it will all work and make a wonderful program that you can be proud of.)

a. WHAT TO LISTEN FOR

You will want statements that address your topic directly, not tangentially. You need several speakers dealing with the same subject, perhaps from different points of view and voicing specific biases, because you need a certain amount of balance in what's being said.

Discard obvious fallacies, outright lies, distortions, and evasions right away — unless you want to make a point; but that is a tricky maneuver. It's best to avoid poor statements early in your editing session.

b. USING YOUR JUDGMENT

To make solid judgments, you have to detach yourself from your own biases and maintain an overview. Realize that you, like most media people, have strong biases, and that you, like us, think what you believe in is inviolate.

Unless you are a polemicist and are being hired as such, your function is to elicit good interviews, to sift through the material, to keep what's good, and to discard what's less well said.

Your editorial judgment is built into the subject you have chosen. For instance, if your topic is the exploitation of a minority, that's already a political statement. The next one is the kind of people you interview. Reserve your bias to these two areas and keep your editorial judgment clear of any political obsession.

The elements you are looking for in interviews and statements are the following —

- Common sense
- Relevance
- Importance
- Consistency
- Quality
- Articulation
- Coherence
- Honesty
- Forthrightness
- Tone of voice

If you find people who will give you an interview and their statements have all these wonderful characteristics, your interviewees are either secular saints, verbal con artists, or they don't exist. No one is that perfect or that good.

So make do with what you can find in a speaker's statement. Use the elements listed above as a guideline only.

Let's look at each characteristic separately.

1. Common sense

When you listen to someone talking on tape, listen not so much to whether the statement appears to be essential to your program but whether or not it makes sense to the average listener. Is it free of buzzwords, or technical jargon?

As the interviewer of professionals and amateurs you have the obligation to make sure statements are intelligible to the lay listener. But do not cater to the intelligence level of the lowest common denominator; occupy the middle ground between an esoteric vocabulary and verbal illiteracy.

What cannot be readily understood must be discarded. In audio productions, the listener cannot go back and reread what was missed the first time. In radio, every statement must be short, simple, precise, and to the point. Common sense is a valuable element of your editorial judgment.

2. Relevance

A statement must be relevant to the general topic, or it won't make it. It's as simple as that. It is your prerogative to edit irrelevant material.

3. Importance

A statement must be important. But what is important to you may not be what was important to the speaker. Importance is a matter of opinion. Does the statement make an impact? Will it sound significant to the listener? You have to do a lot of second-guessing as you edit, and the better you are at that, the more successful your broadcast will be.

4. Consistency

Is what the speaker says consistent? Or has his or her opinion changed so that at the end of the statement the speaker is touting the opposite point of view? (This kind of inconsistent argument is presented more frequently than you would think.)

On the other hand, is the statement too consistent with the speaker's cultural background? Is it stereotypical? Some people will tell you what they believe you want to hear when they make a public statement. They are not hypocrites or liars, they just like to be accommodating. Watch your step. If you're not sure about the cultural habits of citizens in a foreign country, try to study these different attitudes in advance.

5. Quality

Has the statement been well formulated? Does it convey the feeling that the speaker is a person of high standards and fair views? Flippancy can be misinterpreted on tape.

6. Articulation

Can the speaker be understood on tape? Or is the diction so sloppy, or the accents so strong that the meaning gets hidden in an effort to understand what was said? Avoid inarticulate speakers unless they are essential for their expertise. You are discriminating on the basis of enunciation, not on a person's color, race, creed, or political leanings.

7. Coherence

Do all the sentences hang together or are there gaps? A person can be incoherent under stress, when excited, when unaccustomed to expressing abstract thoughts, or when describing disorderly events in an orderly fashion.

8. Honesty

Honesty is a tender area to discuss. Most speakers, if not all, will protest the honesty of their statements. It's up to you to believe them and to make your choice. Your ultimate defense against aggressive speakers who appear to have rented their private version of truth is not to use what they told you. You are under no obligation to do so. Only your conscience is the arbiter here.

9. Forthrightness

Forthrightness is a quality often employed by people who sound authoritative, knowledgeable, and honest. On replaying their statements, without the visual impact of their personality, some statements may sound rather thin. Perhaps there is an attempt at subterfuge, some evasion, a certain bending of the facts somewhere.

10. Tone of voice

Tone of voice is the final tool of editorial judgment you can employ. A voice cannot lie to you. No matter what is said, the tone will give the game away, if there is a game. This kind of judgment in listening comes with experience and is only developed over a number of years. Some people have a talent for judging tone of voice.

c. MAKING THE DECISION

Now you must decide what to keep and what to discard. Your decision will be based on instinct, impulse, focus, and experience.

1. Instinct

You can rely on your instinct when all the other methods of making a decision have failed. Instinct warns you when there's a burglar in your apartment. Instinct tells you to back off or to barge ahead. It is a natural defense.

For our purposes, instinct is guessing whether a speaker's statement on tape will be usable. All good media people have developed their instinct through years of experience and knowledge of their topic. Eventually, you will too. When you begin, your instinct may be off target. Luckily, because you have an outs reel you can always return to what your faulty instinct told you to discard, take it, and add it to the master reel.

2. Impulse

Impulse is a close relative to instinct. It is the little nudge that tells you to go ahead, make a decision, and pick this instead of that statement. We are all acquainted with impulse buying, which is one of the biggest marketing strategies ever devised. Impulsive editing decisions aren't necessarily any better than impulse buying decisions, but they get you away from indecision. After all, making an impulsive decision is not an irreversible action; there is always the outs reel.

3. Focus

Focus means zeroing in on what you want and what you need. Your project must have a focus, or you wouldn't have been able to sell it in the first place. Anything you listen to during your editing session must fit into this focus. If it is tangential, put the statement on the outs reel. Keep only what fits your focus. Later you can go back and pick up fringe material.

4. Experience

You already have some work experience and you are adding to your knowledge all the time. The worst thing to do is to be impatient and lose your temper. Then your judgment will be severely impaired, and your decision will be wrong. Undoing one or two minor mistakes is easy; a whole series of bad judgments will exasperate you. Experience will eventually be a tool of your editorial judgment.

d. START A MASTER TAPE

During the editing session when you pick, save, and discard tape segments to make a master tape, you will be handling tape reels constantly. It's best to stick to one format of seven inches. A seven-inch reel holds, at seven and a half inches per second, thirty or more minutes of tape. They are also lightweight and can be removed from the spindle with ease.

Ten-inch reels are usually metal and must be placed on a special detachable core, which means additional handling every time you change reels. The time to combine two seven-inch reels on a ten-inch reel comes later, when you assemble all the components (see chapter 14).

To compile a master tape, organize your workplace in the following way:

- Place your tape recorder in front of you and at the same height you would keep a typewriter or computer keyboard, so you can reach all the controls without straining. Remove the head cover on your editing tape recorder for easier access to the playback head. You will be changing tape constantly. Also you need to be able to easily mark your tape with a yellow grease pencil.

- Have on hand several empty takeup reels: one reel with blank tape, one with leader tape, and the other reels with the original recordings from which you will work.

- Mount your editing block near or directly underneath the playback head with double-sided adhesive tape. You will have to move marked tape from the playback head to the editing block to make your cut, and you must take the spliced tape from the editing block back to the playback head. There is a lot of such tape handling, and the shorter the distance from recording head to editing block and back, the more time you save.

- Keep all your paraphernalia (the razor blade, the yellow grease pencil, and the splicing tape) to the immediate right of your tape recorder (if you are right-handed). Put the razor blade and the grease pencil on a polyfoam bed so you can grasp them quickly. The closer all your tools are, the fewer movements you waste.

- Keep a pad of lined paper to the right of your blade, grease pencil, and splicing tape. On this pad jot down your synopsized transcript (see subsection i. below).

- Use good quality, open-air headphones to monitor your tape. Most work areas suffer from some environmental noise that will impede your ability to listen closely if you depend on your built-in loudspeaker. Headphones will let you listen without missing a breath or an inflection while you edit the tape.

- You may want to wire your editing tape recorder through the loudspeakers in your home stereo system so you can listen at full volume and in stereo. This is optional; headphones are better.
- Keep a stopwatch and labels handy.

After you have set up your work station, begin assembling your master tape. Don't forget to use one or two seconds worth of leader tape (7 to 15 inches) to separate items.

e. START AN OUTS REEL

After you have listened to the first reel of tape, extracted the items you'll use, and transferred them to the master tape, you will have an outs reel left over. It won't be full, so as you begin to monitor your next reels of tape, add the outs from that one to your first outs reel and continue until it's full. You'll save time when everything has to be put away later if you have all your outs on one reel.

f. KEEP TIME

You want to time the individual sections of your documentary (i.e., segments, inserts, and clips). A segment, or an insert, or a clip is a piece of recorded tape of varying length, complete in itself. Insert is the most commonly used term for a radio documentary, and clip is used for a news item. Segment is the generic term for a clip or an insert.

Keeping these inserts timed will give you an overview of the length of your documentary. Most inserts should be kept well under three minutes. A documentary gains its liveliness from changing interviews, sounds, and music frequently.

You can gauge the overall time by looking at the master tape reel as it fills up. You will soon be able to guess how much time you have. An almost full 7-inch reel at 7-½ ips is 30 minutes of recorded tape.

g. USE LABELS

You are impatient to get going, and you forget to label your tape reels. Time passes and you have forgotten what is what. This can happen in difficult, lengthy assignments with many reels of "recorded," "edited," "discarded," and "maybe" reels.

Establish a system to save yourself from grief. Label the master reels with ID numbers, I, II, III, IV, and so on. Then, because you will have up to three or four seven-inch master tape reels, label them all I-1, I-2, I-3, I-4, and II-1 and so on. Label the outs reels Outs I-1, I-2 and so on; mark the word "outs" in red so as not to confuse the pile.

The labels, of course, should fit the reels. Label or inscribe the boxes as well for faster identification. A good way to inscribe the labels is with the project name, the ID number (I-3 or whatever), the speaker (or speakers), and the recording date. It might look like this:

HOUSING CRISIS I-1
MASTER INSERTS
Jones, Miller, Smith
March, 18, 198-

h. REVISE

Any time you listen to your original tape, you may have second thoughts and wish to revise. If you're not certain that a selection of tape or an insert is the right one, go back right then and there while your impressions are still fresh. Don't wait until later when your second thoughts, and your inspirations, may have disappeared.

i. TRANSCRIBE

Although it will slow down the process of picking, saving, and discarding, you'll save yourself a lot of time if you make a concurrent synopsized transcript. This is the fastest, most accurate and direct way of gaining a detailed overview of an entire radio documentary.

A verbatim transcript is often made of parliamentary or legislative sessions, court trials, hearings, testimonies, impromptu speeches or other such events. It means transcribing every word and it takes a fair amount of effort and time. For our purposes a verbatim transcript is not needed — it's overkill.

But as you listen to a two- to three-minute insert, you need to know its essence, so make a synopsized transcript. On the pad, write the in-cue, the out-cue, the length of the segment, the speaker's name, and the main points raised. It will look like this:

1) "When I Was a Child..."	In France; watching trains go by; waving; yearning; wanted to be sleeping-car conductor; grew up; travelled on trains; wrote book. Had fun.
runs: 1.57	
(Miller)	
"... It Was a Great Event."	

"When I Was a Child" is the in-cue, the first words of an insert. Stop the tape while you write them down. Then as you listen, write words in the right-hand column that help you recall what Mr. Miller said. These trigger words in the right-hand column will tell you quickly what the core of the insert is. Use as many as needed but keep them short.

"Runs" is the time of this insert. The first time you listen, you won't be able to time the insert. It's best to time it the second time around. That will also give you an opportunity to revise your transcript.

"It Was a Great Event" is the out-cue, the last words of this insert. Add the name of the speaker, and you have made your first synopsized transcript.

Number the inserts consecutively so that later they can be easily shuffled as you establish order.

After you have filled your first takeup reel with master tape inserts, go to the next tape (Master Tape I-2) and start a fresh synopsized transcription sheet by marking it accordingly. Learn the habit of identifying everything in sight, because a visual ID is imperative when you handle audio tape that is identifiable only through slow listening.

j. REORGANIZE

Behind the simple word "reorganize" hides the most creative aspect of your documentary project. Reorganizing your inserts means shuffling them like a deck of cards until they come up in the order you need. There is no standard method, but over a number of years I have developed this format, which has served me well.

The organization of a radio documentary is similar to a well-organized newspaper or magazine article. You establish a flow; you tell a story. You might organize your topic into the following sections, as you would a newspaper story. Establish sections and give them capital letters —

    A. Teaser
    B. Introduction
    C. First premise
    D. Second premise
    E. Debate
    F. Balance
    G. Conclusion

(This sample, of course, is without substance and serves only to give you an indication of how you might organize your topic.)

A teaser is a strong opening statement. It may be funny, sad, or controversial. It grabs the listeners' attention, and gets them listening.

Once they're listening, develop your theme. Tell them what they are going to hear in the next few minutes or hour.

Next present the first set of facts and opinions, followed by the second set; then let a debate ensue, perhaps, or whatever presents itself as a section. Coming to the end, try to achieve a balance, and wind up with a conclusion.

Some projects lend themselves to geographical or time sequences. In the documentary on the Orient Express, for example, I began in Paris and ended in Istanbul. If you produce a radio biography, start with your subject's birth and end with his or her death.

But most topics are not so easily organized. Remember that the average listeners' memory is limited and they cannot review your introduction to refresh their memory as they can with a print story. Pause from time to time and repeat what the listeners have just heard in a different context. Reiteration is a legitimate device in radio documentaries.

Now that you have heard and thought about all the inserts twice, your judgment will be vastly improved. Give every insert either one of the capital letters or eliminate it. Now is the time to discard inserts that don't sound right the second time around.

Remember that for a one-hour documentary you might have inserts that run two to two and one half hours. You will have to discard mercilessly. The more experienced you become, the shorter your insert selection will be, and the fewer discards you will face.

k. CONSULT

After you have reorganized all your inserts and constructed a rough master tape, consult your producer.

You can rarely be your own judge and jury; similarly, you can rarely make a radio documentary and hear it broadcast without someone wanting to approve it first. That's fair enough. The people who buy your original idea for a radio documentary want to know what you've done before they let it air. And you'll be lucky if you have to deal only with one producer.

Once the master tape is ready, seek your producer's approval of what you have done so far. Make an appointment well in advance and give your producer enough time to listen to your program before discussing it with you.

When you involve your producer at this early stage, you make three wise moves. First, you recognize the authority of his or her position and, consequently, you avoid offending his or her potentially sensitive ego. Flattery always works. If your producer has any suggestions, write them down.

Second, you gain your producer's commitment to your project and he or she will encourage you to go ahead and finish your work. If your producer is committed to your project you can be reasonably sure you'll be home free as you finish the program. You will have tied down the loose ends that might otherwise have tripped you up.

Third, you engage an objective listener. Your producer might discover a contradiction in your quotes. If that is the case, now is the time to clarify the matter. Consult the interviewee and record another interview if necessary.

l. SUMMING UP

All this may sound like a lot of work; it is. But remember that there are few freelance assignments (or salaried jobs, for that matter) more satisfying than producing a radio documentary. It calls on so many levels of expertise that, as a radio documentarist, you are like a one-person band playing dozens of instruments with equal dexterity.

13

THE SECRET OF EDITING

Editing audio tape is not a mechanical job, nor it is dull and repetitive work; on the contrary, it's a fine art. When you have learned to be a creative tape editor, you will be well on the way to becoming competent at researching, preparing, and assembling a radio program of any kind. Unless you are a good tape editor, you will not be a good radio documentarist.

There are three reasons why you should edit audio tape. First, you want to choose statements or sounds you think are relevant and discard the rest; second, you want to edit tape down to the length of time your program dictates; third, you want to improve what was recorded without changing its meaning. Now that you have learned the difficult process of picking, saving, and discarding tape segments, you can be concerned with the physical aspect of editing.

a. TECHNIQUE

Make sure you have an editing block, leader tape, splicing tape, razor blade, yellow grease pencil, several takeup reels, and a stopwatch. These are your editing tools. Keep your hands as clean and dry as possible. Avoid touching the oxide side of the tape — human skin is almost always greasy and leaves prints.

The technique of editing consists of listening for what you want to extract, marking the tape at the beginning and the end of this segment, making the two corresponding cuts, transferring the segment to where you want it on the master tape, and inserting it by splicing both ends to the master tape. To edit in this fashion, you must use reel-to-reel quarter-inch audio tape. Audio cassette tapes cannot be edited this way. Although you can, after a fashion, edit cassette audio tape electronically by dubbing to another cassette recorder, the process takes far too much time and is too involved. This is the main reason why the handier cassettes have not replaced reel-to-reel tape.

1. Listening

Listen to find the exact place where you want to make your cut. This spot should be relatively silent so that the tape sounds natural and not obviously edited when you join the segments together. The ideal place to mark tape for a cut is at the beginning of a speaker's sentence and at its end (see section c. below).

2. Marking

It is best to mark the tape with a yellow grease pencil that will stand out against the brown audio tape. There are two ways of marking:

(a) Mark a vertical yellow stroke directly on the tape surface that covers the playback head. This method is very accurate, but crude, and not recommended. Playback heads are precision tools and putting pressure and grease on them can shorten their life.

(b) On most tape recorders you will find a rigid surface not far from the playback head. Measure the distance between playback head and marking surface and transfer it to your editing block. This will enable you to make precise marks. If the marking surface is seven-eighths of an inch to the right of the playback head, mark off seven-eighths of an inch to the right of your 45° or 60° cutting slot on the editing block.

Before you make your first cut, you should know where your second cut will be, indicating the end of your selected piece of tape. Mark the beginning and end.

3. Cutting

The most convenient razor blades to use for cutting audio tape are those available in hair cutting supply stores. They are about two inches long, five-eighths of an inch wide, and have only one cutting edge. The other edge is protected to prevent injuries.

Smooth the tape into the groove of the editing block with your finger tip and move the yellow grease mark to the cutting slot. Then slice the tape, don't saw. Use economical movements that won't hack the aluminum sides of the cutting slot. And as soon as the razor blade gets dull, replace it. Dull cuts create jagged edges that won't join smoothly. Precision and neatness are essential to precise and neat editing cuts.

When you have made your cut, grab the tape at both ends of the block and snap it out. If you just pull or jerk, the tape may stretch and distort the sound.

4. Transferring

On a separate reel, assemble the pieces of tape you want to keep, and separate them with short lengths of leader tape. Leader tape is a light color (often white), and helps you find a specific tape segment when you rewind your tape or run it fast forward.

5. Splicing

For convenience's sake, put your roll of splicing tape on the core of a heavy office-type tape dispenser so you can tear off pieces on the jagged edge.

Join the two tape ends together on your editing block, pressing them down firmly so you can push them together until they just touch. Take an inch-long piece of splicing tape and place it over the two ends. Avoid touching the sticky side. Grease from your fingers will reduce the splicing tape's adhesive quality, and it might cause the two ends to separate while the tape is running forward or being rewound at high speed. Use your finger tip or finger nail to tamp down the splicing tape until it bonds firmly with the audio tape.

Unless you take your time to secure the splicing tape, you will experience a most distressing accident: while rewinding your tape at high speed, the splice will come apart, and tape will fly all over the studio floor. You would have to spend considerable time untangling the mess if this happened. Firm splices are a must.

b. ROUGH EDIT

You can do either a rough or a fine edit. The first editing session is a rough edit in which you select chunks of material, put them in sequence, and don't worry about timing, awkward pauses, *um*s and *ah*s, repetitions, sloppy transitions, or other flaws. These rough edges can stay in until the fine editing session.

Before fine editing, though, go through your rough-edited master tape for the second time. You might have to throw away some segments, and you don't want to waste time fine editing these.

A rough-edited version of the master tape should be a few minutes longer than the finished product. You will lose several minutes when you fine edit the master and take out all those hesitations and repeated words.

c. FINE EDIT

1. Sentences

When editing an interview or statement, you will find sentences that can be cut without altering the speaker's central message. Consider for a moment a typical TV newsclip, in which editing is only possible by electronic means, and where it's considered a mortal sin to have the picture jump because of an internal edit. When a speaker hesitates, or mispronounces a word, or uses an excessive amount of *um*s and *ah*s, there's nothing an editor can do except cut the speaker off. And this is what happens. Speakers get chopped off in mid-sentence, even with the inflection rising — bad editing at its worst.

In radio, you have more latitude. It is possible to keep the beginning of a sentence, edit the center portion, and keep the last bit. It is also possible to rearrange the parts. It will still sound as if the speaker said it that way.

But I have found that it's better to use whole sentences, and just clean them up internally. I take out all the verbal junk but leave the message intact. Otherwise, the product can be too dense to follow.

One reason for using whole sentences is that many speakers end their sentences with a rising inflection. That makes editing difficult. Professional announcers end every phrase or sentence with a falling inflection, which sounds more natural. As well, you can edit anywhere without letting the words hang in the air, waiting. Rising inflections are deadly habits, but you are stuck with them. You can't manipulate inflected words within a sentence, hence it is easier to use whole sentences.

You can, however, cut off a sentence's false beginning to save a precious amount of air time. A false beginning is a speaker's way of finding time to think; for example, "As I was saying just the other day, and I believe it can be repeated without infringing in the least on the rights in question. . . . Anyway, I believe it's safe to say that in my humble opinion, and without wanting to cast aspersions against anyone . . . that after due consideration, thousands of birds in the Bahamas are in danger of becoming extinct."

Although this sample is exaggerated, most speakers back into their statements with unnecessary verbiage. Take it out. In the example above, you would begin the edited version with "Thousands of birds. . .," and carry on from there.

Similarly, academics, some politicians, and many professional speakers will first tell you what they are going to talk about, then make the statement, and finally summarize what they have just said. Very often the summary is the best statement of the three. Keep that intact, use it, and consign the other two versions to your outs reel.

When editing a statement on tape, make sure the background noise matches. If not, you will make an obvious edit; for example, if you have someone talking while an aircraft is flying overhead and you edit a portion of their statement, when the speaker resumes, suddenly the aircraft will be gone. Then the listener will know the tape has been edited, which is what you want to avoid.

Also be aware of a speaker's pace. Sometimes it is hectic; sometimes it is too relaxed. Edit dead air gaps or insert pauses until the listening pace is just right. You won't have altered the message, just its rhythm.

2. Words

The editing rule for words is different. Many interviewees have a habit of starting wrong, stopping, and starting again. Or they stop in mid-word and do not finish their sentences. Or they mispronounce a word, stop, and repeat the word at a markedly higher volume.

In all these cases it's good policy to clean up verbal faults. They may be overlooked in the face-to-face conversation because the speaker's presence distracts you; the visual somehow attenuates the poor audio; you tend to forgive the speaker's bad grammar, lousy syntax, half-words, and mispronunciations when you are with the speaker. But when you are only listening, all these faults are intensified. You must edit them.

Should you have to eliminate a word or half-word, though, and another word follows that doesn't connect smoothly, introduce a pause so the pacing isn't off. Sometimes a pause is not enough, and the word still sounds chopped. Then add a sudden sound, such as a door closing, to bridge the gap. A good editor can make the tape sound as if the mistake never occurred.

Here's another secret: Remember the speakers who repeat a stumbled or mispronounced word to help you in editing except that almost always they repeat the word differently — louder, more accentuated, whatever, and the repeated word becomes unusable? To edit their mistake you can go hunting for the identical word in a segment on your outs reel. That's why you keep every piece of tape until the project is together. Discarded outs are a treasure trove of duplicate words. Isolate a duplicate of the word you want to replace, compare its inflection and background noise with the segment you are editing, then cut out the word, and transfer it to the master tape.

3. Ums and ahs

"Thinking sounds" are the tape editor's scourge. Even some of the most accomplished intellectuals use *ums* and *ahs* so frequently that, as the editor who must cut these *ums* and *ahs*, you will want to strangle anyone who uses them.

But *ums* and *ahs* are a defensive mechanism most people aren't even aware they use. When they speak, their thoughts are simply too slow for their faster mouths. Such speakers stop in mid-sentence, searching for words to struggle out of the gray cells, through the central nervous system, and into the muscles that operate jaws, tongue, and lips.

Instead of just stopping to think, these speakers feel they must say something, so they say something like this: "When . . . um . . . I . . . went to . . . ah . . . Timbuktoo the other day . . . um . . . no . . . ah . . . wasn't it? . . . Let's see, . . . um . . . the . . . the . . . yes, it was . . . um . . . the other mo-month. . . ."

To make a statement sound normal and fluent, the tape editor has an obligation to correct a speaker's speech pattern if his or her *ums* and *ahs* become frequent and disturbing. A few are allowed; use your judgment.

4. Breaths

Audible breathing is another enemy of the tape editor. Some speakers breathe noisily and make a production of it. Others, for example, most professional announcers, breathe almost inaudibly.

The sound of taking a breath before making a statement does not add to the acoustic value of what is about to be said. Unless the first word is explosive or doesn't sound right without the indrawn breath, edit the breath out. Who needs it?

On the other hand, leave breaths between words. In-drawn breaths within a long sentence are necessary, otherwise the listener will start a bit of substitute breathing for the speaker out of sympathy for his or her discomfort.

And be very careful when you delete a sentence that you don't wind up with a double breath. That happens all the time. But if it does occur, you should catch your error at the fine-edit stage. It is something to listen for.

5. Rhythm and pauses

Rhythm is a sibling of pacing. Experienced speakers have an established speaking rhythm. One element of rhythm, the dramatic pause, can be very effective when talking to a crowd. During a radio interview, however, it is nothing but dead air. Take it out, shorten it, and follow your speaker's normal rhythm.

With speakers who have no sense of rhythm, you may be forced to add or remove pauses here and there. This kind of task is what makes editing such a creative job. You may be called upon to reconstruct a speaker's statement. As long as you don't change the meaning or the intent, you are entitled to correct the rhythm. Again, this is a matter of editorial judgment.

d. TIMING

Let's assume you have finished your master tape. Your producer asked you to provide 18.45 minutes, but your program is 21.23 minutes. You must edit to bring it down to the required time.

Novices will often argue that any further edit is impossible and the production is already down to its bare minimum. There are two problems with this attitude.

First, you must always be aware of time. Throughout the fine edit, keep a running check on the accumulated time. Even then you may end up with more than you anticipated. Continue to edit pauses, to cut *ums* and *ahs*, to delete repetitions, to modify statements, and to shorten your script.

Second, keep in mind that nothing is sacrosanct. The earlier you realize that the world will not grind to a halt because a 21.23 minute production must be trimmed to 18.45 minutes, the better.

You have two devices for timing audio tape — the stopwatch and the tape recorder. Use them. The new studio tape recorders have built-in tape counters that read minutes and seconds very quickly.

e. SAVING OUTS

Saving every last scrap of tape on an outs reel is important, as you now know from learning to match mispronunciations and half-words. When you've finished an assignment, you should have the following tape reels to add to your collection:

- Master tape
- General outs
- Final outs
- Pauses, *ums,* and *ah*s

Some documentarists also call the master tape "inserts." Inserts, which you separate with leader tape, are the segments that will make up the master tape after you add readings, narration, SFX, and music.

General outs are the interviews or SFX not used on the master tape. They are what is left on the original reel after you've written "outs" on the label, preferably in red.

Final outs come out of the master tape in the fine-editing process. Keep them on a separate reel and label it clearly.

A pauses and *ums and ah*s outs reel is an option. Certainly dead air pauses can be useful, and some documentarists take a devilish delight in splicing together all their *um*s and *ah*s, false starts, half-words, and mispronunciations for a few minutes of entertainment on dull winter evenings. Just make sure that such irreverent mementoes are clearly labeled and identified so they don't get aired by mistake.

f. STEREO JUMPS

Stereo jumps are accidents that can mar a stereo production. Listen for them as you replay your master tape. A stereo jump occurs when you make a 45° splice in a spot where there isn't absolute or relative silence. Absolute silence is the absence of any ambient noise; relative silence is the presence of low background noise (not enough to matter).

When you cut through a piece of recorded tape at a 45° angle, on playback the leading edge of the cut arrives at the right playback head, then the left (see Figure #11). You will hear the same sound jump from the right to the left loudspeaker. This is a stereo jump, an annoying phenomenon, but unless you find a dead spot to splice, you cannot avoid it.

There are ways around a stereo jump, but none solves the problem. If the stereo jump isn't too pronounced, try a 60° cut, eliminating much of the leading edge. If you have very strong splicing tape, try a 90° cut, but you risk breaking the vertical splice later. The best way to prevent stereo jumps is to make your 45° cut at an absolutely silent spot on the tape.

g. SUMMING UP

While you are learning to edit audio tape, you may be tempted to rush or to despair. Neither is good for the product or for your soul. Realize that editing is slow at first. You have to learn what to do and how to do it well before you can do it quickly. Go slowly at first, and one day you will breeze along at a dizzying speed. Once you gain confidence, even creative editing becomes routine. But that doesn't take away from the joy of ending up with a fine product that sounds good.

FIGURE #11
STEREO JUMP

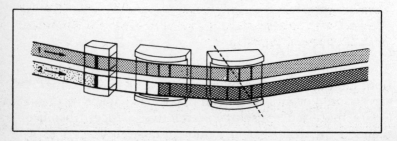

14

ASSEMBLING ALL COMPONENTS

You now have all the components for your radio documentary ready for constructing your master tape, the penultimate step to the broadcast tape.

Your script holds together all the components — inserts, music, SFX, readings, and bits of research. (See the Appendix for a sample script.) Then, all the components are put in order and connected through the narration (see chapter 15).

a. REVIEW YOUR COMPONENTS

Your perspective may have changed from conception to completion and you may have some new ideas. Review your tape. Put yourself in your listeners' position and tell them your story. Do you catch their interest right away? Then do you give them an overview of what to expect? Do you manage to organize your thoughts on tape so everything begins at the beginning and ends at the end?

Or, if there is no clear beginning, do you develop your premise, prove your point, contest it, shake it up, put it back together, and finally come to a conclusion that makes sense?

If your ideas all seem to work, you have the basic structure for your radio documentary. Now add music, SFX and narration to this frame to make your edifice of thoughts and ideas self-supporting.

b. CHECK YOUR FACTS

A well constructed radio documentary is like a fortress, unassailable because all the facts are documented and in their proper place. Your quotes are solid and authoritative.

If you render your radio documentary's structure earth-quake-proof, your subject matter can be as rattling to your listeners as you want it to be. Your documentary won't collapse and bury you beneath the rubble of slapdashery. You will prove yourself competent and trustworthy.

In radio, establishing your credibility early in your career is not only desirable, it is essential to more assignments. The media landscape is littered with the figurative corpses of young, brash, talented reporters, writers and documentarists who wanted success too fast and cut corners, bent facts, invented situations, intimidated people, and ignored other aspects. These failures had an idea, added a flimsy angle, began to build a story, discovered the facts wouldn't hold up under scrutiny, but rather than scrap the documentary, they doctored it and got caught with their facts down.

When you review the components that make up your master tape, double-check not only their sequence but whether or not the facts hold up. Hang on to any proof you have collected well past the time you think you may need it.

c. ATTRIBUTE QUOTATIONS

Every fact must be nailed down. Consider the five Ws — the credo of every journalist — Who? What? When? Where? Why?

You must be concerned with who said whatever was said. But how do you establish someone's identification (ID) on radio? In print it's easy. You may glance across an attribution and forget the name of the person quoted when you are reading. Then if you later want to know who said what, you just reread the last few sentences or paragraphs, and there is the name.

In radio, the rules are different. Here the speaker's and the statement's importance governs whether or not it is identified. When a disgruntled passerby says old-age pension should be reduced, it's a different story than when a senator, who has social and political clout, says the same thing.

People who hold public office or other high profile jobs are likely to influence the lives of others. Their quotes should be identified right away, every time they say something. A passerby can be assumed to be *vox populi*, someone expressing an opinion, but not someone whose identity is of immediate interest to anyone but family or friends.

The importance of the statement is another factor that guides whether or not you attribute a quote. If a passerby advocates a social program of stunning insight and convincing depth, that person should be identified.

As a rule, though, anyone who says something on radio ought to be identified, if only as a matter of courtesy.

There are four places in a radio program to attribute quotes:

- Before the statement
- During the statement
- After the statement
- At the end of the program

(See chapter 15, Writing the Narration, for the precise technique.)

d. ADD READINGS

Review your master tape for places to insert the quotations you gathered in your research. (Quotations become readings after they are recorded.)

A quotation must be placed where it enhances a speaker's statement, or where it clarifies an earlier point.

Alternatively, a quotation can be inserted as transition between two disjointed statements. A well-read quotation will perk up the listeners' interest just because it changes the atmosphere. The reader, usually an actor, adds a distinctive voice to the master tape.

A quote can also be employed as a voice-over, to be added as a second layer of sound. American film director Robert Altman excels in the use of dialogue that runs over itself: two people talking simultaneously, the way it happens in life all the time. In radio, this technique can be used in a limited way. Music, sound effects, and narration can be combined in ever increasing numbers until the message is garbled. Be careful with voice-overs because they may render the rest of the signal unintelligible.

e. ADD SPACES

At first thought, adding spaces may not make sense to you. But think again. You need spaces throughout the master tape where you can place IDs, readings, and narration.

A space is created by bringing the previous statement, sound effect or music excerpt to an obvious close, however temporary. Listen for a natural pause, usually following a falling inflection, as you would when editing sentences (see chapter 13, section c.).

Mark the spaces you find with leader tape of a different color. Then write down the out and in cues, so you know what goes where. Remember that one piece of tape looks like the other. Identify every piece. Know what's what, where it goes, and how you can find the spot again.

f. ADD SOUND EFFECTS

Sound effects can be added as a separate layer under or over speech tracks. But when you want to use SFX as an illustrative, descriptive, or even dramatic segment in your program, you must find a space in which to put them, so the same rules apply.

If you have cleverly recorded SFX of the right duration, with proper fade-in and fade-out, splice them into your master tape at this time.

You may, of course, not be able to splice SFX in a particular spot, because the insert is too long, or perhaps because it begins with a bang and ends with a chop where you would prefer to use a gentle fade-in and fade-out. In this case, just insert a leader tape where the SFX should go, and write the in and out cues into your script. Your sound engineer can make adjustments to the SFX during the final montage.

110

Or, use the hard cut as a device to make a statement with your sound. I once prepared a radio feature on Martin Luther in which this technique was used to great advantage. The sound engineer cut abruptly into the tempest section of Beethoven's Sixth Symphony, then to the plaintive cry of young Luther as he lay winded and stunned by a bolt of lightning. The sequence — thundering music, cut, plaintive cry, cut, thundering music — worked very well, because the hard cuts created drama.

While this is a legitimate practice, don't use it too much or you will repeat yourself and kill the effect.

g. ADD MUSIC

Your music inserts will be added later, during the final montage, unless you happen to have the music you need on tape and it's the right duration. But if you splice music into the master tape, you won't benefit from the sound engineer's expertise, which means you limit your experimental parameters unnecessarily.

As a rule, the sound engineer can manipulate music inserts taken from records or compact discs more easily in the studio than you can on the master tape. All you must do, then, is insert leader tape where the music should go, and write the in and out cues into the script.

h. KEEP TIME

You can tell approximately how long your documentary runs by looking at how much tape you have assembled. But that goes only for the tape. You must also leave room for IDs, readings, SFX, music, and narration. You must guess their times, or use a general rule of thumb: In a one-hour radio documentary or feature, you can expect to use 40 minutes of tape inserts, meaning interviews and statements, and 20 minutes of written material, SFX, and music. But that is only a very rough guideline.

Keep time throughout the assembly process as you weigh individual components. After a while, you will acquire a feeling for the length of each one.

15

WRITING THE NARRATION

Once you have assembled all the components that constitute a radio documentary, established their sequence,
marked spaces for other inserts, identified every piece of
tape including the spaces between inserts (in and out cues),
timed everything so you won't have too much adding or
cutting to do later, you are ready to write the narration.

By this time, you should have a rough script. Now it's
cut-and-paste time, unless you use your computer screen
to revise the script and insert narration.

a. THREE RULES

Before you begin to write your narration, be aware that all
the writing skills you have acquired privately or in a learning institution have been directed toward expressing your
thoughts and ideas on paper, in written form. By definition, radio is the antithesis of the written word. The
spoken word is governed by completely different rules.

In this chapter you will learn a new way of expressing
yourself. You will learn to write a sentence that sounds
good read aloud, but is not necessarily elegant on paper.

1. Consider your listener

First, become aware of your ability to listen. Observe your
habits. Are you able to let your conversation partner finish
before you give in to your compulsion to speak? Observe
others as they listen to you. Notice that most people let
their eyes wander and purse their lips, indicating they
cannot wait for you to finish so they can sound off.

I use two devices to avoid my listeners' attention wandering. I examine what I'm saying as I speak. Why is it boring
the listener? Is the subject too esoteric? Is the language too

complex? Is the topic alien or offensive? Am I being too long-winded? If so, I quickly change my tack, or I end my spiel.

Also, I employ a dirty trick or two to regain someone's attention. I will suddenly stop in mid-sentence. That jars the listener back to what I was saying. Or, if the listener has been rude, looking around, focusing attention on someone else, I will say, "You're not paying attention to me," upon which the listener feels guilty, apologizes, and makes a point of appearing keen and interested in my words.

The first analytical method is better because it's non-aggressive. It assumes that you, the speaker, may have goofed somewhere. The second method is useful when you feel you have to retaliate. It works, but it isn't nice.

Keeping these listening habits in mind, imagine the listener scanning the radio dial, trying to find something other than mindless music. The listener comes to your program and hears a ponderous exposition read badly and dully by you. The listener will twirl the knob, and wander on.

The main point of any narration in a radio program is to sound lively and interesting. You may have the most exciting documentary on your hands, but if you fail to connect the components with a narration that meets the standard of your program, you will fail.

2. Hire a good narrator

The second rule of good narration is to decide who should read it on the air. In most cases, leave the narration to professionals. There are conflicting opinions on this, but I have heard too many documentaries (including some of my own early ones) that the writer narrated. The result: The narration was difficult to listen to. Make it easy on yourself, hire a pro.

3. Keep in short

The third rule of good narration is to keep it short. Let the people you have interviewed speak instead. A lot of narration is superfluous and serves only to inflate the opinion radio documentarists often have of themselves. It's far more valid to establish a mood than to describe ideas in numbing detail. Details are forgotten as soon as they are aired.

As a guideline, use fewer angles per broadcast, short bursts of explanatory narration, short sentences and simple words.

Some repetition is helpful, however, especially when simplifying a thought weakens its impact. Then repeat what has just been said, but in another context. Good public speakers follow this rule all the time. Announce what you will talk about, do it, and summarize what you've said.

Ideally you shouldn't have to write a narration; be spontaneous. But whether you decide to write your narration in detail, or plan to extemporize some of it, remember to keep it short.

b. TELL A STORY

As you begin writing your narration, you will be uncomfortably aware of how much there is to say, and how very few minutes you have in which to say it. You are the victim of information overload, and — instead of cutting it down to size — you want to unload it on your listeners. Quash the inner panic of thinking you have too much information to convey in too short a time. Your narration only sketches the story; the other elements of your broadcast fill it in.

Introduce your narration in a simple and straightforward style. Tell the listeners what you imagine they will want to hear in a way they will understand. This is not catering to the lowest common denominator. On the contrary, never assume your listeners are any less intelligent than you are; never condescend.

To a certain extent, though, as you begin writing the narration, you must simplify the complexity of your program. Trim the information to fewer and fewer points, perhaps to only one or two. If you are telling someone's life story, pick the most interesting and entertaining events in that person's life, not what you think are its most important stations. Make use of anecdotes rather than analysis, of a story line rather than an editorial, of a parable rather than a harangue, and of a simple tale rather than a complex philosophical edifice.

If listeners have to concentrate too hard to follow the story in your radio documentary, they will wander off. Pace your narration: fast, slow, pause. Accelerate, slow down, backtrack a little, repeat an aspect if need be, carry on, and be funny, then serious.

As well, stick to your story line. Set one foot in front of the other, but never start running, or you will leave them behind.

c. READ ALOUD

Once you have written the introduction to your narration, usually the most difficult part, read it aloud, or, if you can, ask someone to read it for you.

Allow for the nonprofessional reading, but listen closely to how your narration sounds. Never mind the elegant sentence that carries on over four full lines. Do you have to listen twice to understand what was said? If so, it is time to rewrite.

Continue to monitor your narration by reading aloud, paragraph by paragraph.

d. PROVIDE TRANSITIONS

A good, short narration will be used primarily to provide transitions from one component to the next. Write connecting script, or use short sound effects or pieces of music to gain time, to pause, to reflect, or to introduce a new aspect of the story.

e. USE SHORT SENTENCES

You could get away with writing long sentences for your narrations if you kept them clear and sequential. But there's no need. Alternate between short and punchy sentences, and longer, more contemplative ones for a good narration.

As a rule, introduce one subject per sentence, or continue developing the same thought sentence by sentence, not all in one long compound sentence. Using too many *ands* is the subterfuge of a lazy writer.

The inherent danger of writing very short sentences is a staccato effect that loses continuity. Experiment. Change pace and direction. But always remember to write as you would talk to a person.

f. CHOOSE SIMPLE WORDS

Showing off your erudition is everyone's prerogative and secret vice. In writing text, you may get away with it, but not on the air.

The rule is simple. If you write "She took a Gadarene plunge" to describe someone's fatal jump, the reader can consult a dictionary and return to the passage. But if "Gadarene plunge" is heard on the air, the listener has no time to look it up. You may, in using this somewhat archaic and rarely used expression, frustrate your listeners if they lose the story's continuity because a word distracts them.

When you record an interview with an erudite (educated sounds better on the air) person, for example, and that person uses an esoteric (obscure sounds better) expression, interrupt the person and ask for an immediate definition. Not only does that flatter the speaker, but it means you don't have to add an explanation in your narration when you introduce the speaker on tape.

Using simple words in a narration is not an insult to listeners, it is a courtesy and common sense.

g. REWRITE HYPERBOLE

There is too much hyperbole, or exaggeration, in too many radio broadcasts. Rewrite to erase excess language from your narration. Even the sentences of respected authors should be rewritten and simplified. But don't change the central message, or you will get irate calls and letters, or worse. If the hyperbole is excessive, discard the author's quotation and pick someone else's.

h. RESPECT COPYRIGHT

All published authors are the owners of copyright in their works for a period of 50 years after their death. Then their work enters the public domain and is free to be used. Until then, you must painstakingly record all the quotations you use and write to the publishers for permission to use them. Occasionally, you will have to pay to use an excerpt.

In cases of foreign text translated into English, even if the authors may long be dead, any contemporary translations are governed by the same 50-year ownership rules.

Should you ever be tempted to circumvent this law, think twice before you give in. Remember that you own the rights to your broadcast, at least to the interviews you have conducted, and you own the rights to your narration. You would not want them to be used without your permission. It is simply considerate to write for permission and pay for the material you use, and it keeps you away from legal hassles.

i. PLACE IDs

As mentioned in chapter 14, there are four places to identify a speaker:

- Before the statement
- During the statement
- After the statement
- At the end of the program

An ID need not be elaborate. You might say, for instance, "Professor Bill Smith teaches anthropology at the University of Uttar Pradesh." Then you place this ID before he speaks.

Or, you wait until there's a natural break in his speech pattern. Already you have placed a leader tape here, duly noting on your scratch pad the in and out cues:

> TAPE ENDS: ". . . and then he vanished into oblivion."
>
> [ID goes here]
>
> TAPE BEGINS: "So, when she started thinking again. . ."

You could also place the ID at the end of the statement. Or, during the credits, you could list all the speakers, and thank them.

If some speakers are used several times during a broadcast, simply say: "Professor Smith again," or, "Once more, Professor Smith."

j. ADD CREDITS

Tell your listeners who prepared the broadcast, who produced it, who the sound engineers were, who read the narration, and who read the quotations. Also mention the institutions and organizations that assisted you. Any other acknowledgments can be elegantly stated at the end of the narration and of the broadcast.

k. SUMMING UP

Now that your narration is written, your radio documentary is about to be produced. The time has come to whip it into shape via the final montage, the packaging session in the studio with the expertise of the producer and the sound engineer.

16

THE FINAL MONTAGE

In radio, a montage, sometimes called packaging, is the construction of an audio sequence in the studio. It involves a few people: the writer (you), a producer, a sound engineer, the actors who voice the readings, and an announcer.

Your role is largely passive now the script is written. The person in charge of a montage is the producer. In cases where you have contracted to deliver a finished radio documentary, you are in charge and function as your own producer.

a. COMPLETE THE SCRIPT

The finished script should contain the following components:

- Tape inserts
- Narration
- Readings
- Sound effects
- Music
- Credits

Sample #2 shows the format for a regular two-track stereo script for the final montage.

For complex and ambitious multi-track documentaries, construct a visual aid for the sound engineer. Although a sound graph is not a stringent requirement, listing the different tracks helps the recording sound engineer determine where the components are located on the 16-track tape recorder. Experienced sound engineers can put together a complex production without a visual aid. (See Sample #3.)

119

SAMPLE #2
A FINAL SCRIPT

NARRATOR: We want to tell you about Bill and Theresa, and how they managed to survive in the wilderness after their plane crash-landed. It was a stormy . . .

SFX: WIND AND DRIVING RAIN, SNEAK UNDER, KEEP UP

NARRATOR: . . . day in Alaska's wilds when the light airplane's engine started to sputter, then conked out. . .

SFX: SIMULATED AIRCRAFT ENGINE FAILURE, SNEAK UNDER, THEN ESTABLISH UNTIL SIMULATED CRASH

SFX: SUDDEN SILENCE PUNCTUATED BY DRIPPING, THEN A WHOOSH, INDICATING FLAMES, ROAR OF FIRE

TAPE 2: BEGINS: Men seek for seclusion in the. . .
RUNS: .56
ENDS: . . . to which you must return

TAPE 1: BEGINS: I said to her, my God, Theresa, are you. . .
RUNS: 1.46
ENDS: . . . first thing was to find food

MUSIC: BEETHOVEN'S SIXTH (SOLTI) SIDE 2 CUT 3 RAPID FADE-IN, ESTABLISH, FADE-OUT ON CUE

NARRATOR: The couple was stranded for 57 days and 17 hours, and what kept them alive was their woodcraft, their good physical shape, and their . . . well, . . . listen to what Theresa has to say on that.

TAPE 1: BEGINS: It was our faith in God, that's all. . .
RUNS: 2.39
ENDS: . . . was to go to our church and thank God

MUSIC: BACH'S 'NUN DANKET ALLE GOTT' SIDE 1 CUT 6. SNEAKS UNDER PREVIOUS TAPE ON CUE THEN UP

SFX: FADE-IN UNDER MUSIC: SOUNDS OF WALKING, BIRDSONG; FADE-OUT MUSIC ON CUE, SFX UP THEN FADE-OUT ON CUE

NARRATOR: We've heard that Bill and Theresa survived their ordeal in the wilds of Alaska, that faith and their survival skills were the reasons they were alive when a search plane saw that mark in the clearing, the large sign spelling H-E-L-P. But the odds were against them, as Professor Walter Harris of the University of Alaska says. He has interviewed Bill and Theresa, and he thinks:

TAPE 1: BEGINS: Really, they had a very small chance. . .
RUNS: 3.17
ENDS: . . . almost too difficult to believe for me

NARRATOR: Professor Harris admits he is skeptical but. . .

Sample #2 demonstrates the dramatic use of sound effects and musical elements. Where you read "on cue" the studio producer would signal the sound engineer what to do with the sounds and the music. "Sneak under" also called "crossfade" or "segue," means to gradually increase from zero volume to the volume level desired. "Tape 1" refers to the master tape on which all the recorded interviews are assembled in order. "Tape 2" is a collection of readings; the quote used here is from Marcus Aurelius' Meditations, Book Four, paragraph 3. (See the Appendix for a sample of another script.)

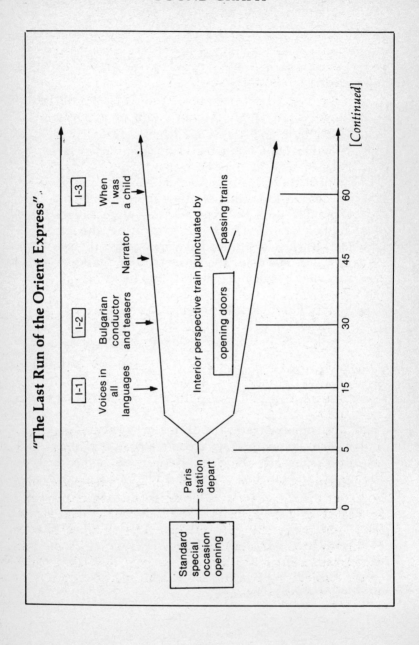

"The Last Run of the Orient Express"

b. PREPARE FOR PRODUCTION

When you come to the final montage, there are many variables. Here are a few points to keep in mind:

- The best way to orchestrate your final script for the montage is to listen to other radio documentaries and features as often as you can. You will detect a pattern worth emulating yourself.

- Tape inserts of interviews should generally be no longer than three or four minutes. Remember to change your pace.

- A loose rule is that sound effects should last no longer than 30 seconds. Whether or not SFX should be kept audible underneath spoken passages depends entirely on content. Sometimes they should be, but not for more than 30 to 45 seconds. This is an area that can be kept flexible.

- There are no rules for using music under spoken passages to illustrate or dramatize, but always keep it shorter than you would like. Restraint in the use of special effects is always wise.

- Any readings should generally be kept shorter than a minute, but they can be longer in exceptional circumstances. Keep everything as concise as you can.

- Alternate components in a documentary or feature (i.e., taped inserts, interviews, readings, SFX, music) as often as possible without affecting the flow of the story.

Finally, remember that in radio you have a vast advantage over the printed word. You can change the pace and the voices just by juggling the components.

In the montage, your role is that of a composer who puts together a musical score to be performed by the instrumentalists and the soloists. The final script is your score. The montage is the performance. The studio producer (who may be you as well) functions as the conductor. Your taped inserts, the narration, the readings, the SFX, and the music bridges or inserts are the instruments and the soloists of your orchestra.

c. CONSULT STUDIO PROFESSIONALS

In the studio, your theoretical construction will undergo the acid test of reality — the transition from how you think it should sound to how it actually sounds when the montage is complete and you have a broadcast tape ready to be aired. If you are lucky, you will have the help of a creative studio producer, or at least a creative sound engineer who knows music and sounds. It's always desirable to bounce ideas off people whose judgment you trust. Their advice will help you produce a better documentary.

d. RECHECK THE TIMING

The last job is to do the final timing and trim the broadcast tape to size. If you have been conscientious in timing the master tape and the other components all along, trimming here and there, you might come up with a broadcast tape that is close to the requisite time limit.

If you need additional material, rework some of the sequences, rewrite your script, record more narration, or include more interview inserts from your outs tapes.

It is much better for your timing to be fat, meaning you are two or three minutes over the time limit. Then you can trim seconds here and there until your production is exactly on time.

When you have completed the montage, make a dub. Copy the broadcast tape immediately as a backup, as you would your computer discs. Keep the copy in a different place from the original to protect against fire, theft, misplacement, water damage or excessive humidity and heat.

17
SUMMING UP

a. PULLING IT ALL TOGETHER

None of the skills described in this book comes easily. Some are based on common sense; others are the product of inspiration and perseverance. Throughout this book I have assumed that you have innate talent for the work of writing and producing radio dramas, features, docu-dramas, and documentaries. That talent just needed developing.

Once you have acquired the skills used to write and produce a radio documentary, you can apply them in related fields. Once you know how to think like a professional radio journalist, you can learn to write by acquiring a few additional skills. You may wish to experiment with creative sound in radio for a few years, and then apply yourself to television. Then you could exchange your microphone and camera for a word processor, and churn out plays, TV drama, movies, whatever. None of the skills you have learned will ever be superfluous.

But do remember to be organized and get going under your own power, without depending on the discipline imposed by a workplace and a superior who tells you to get started. Be a self-starter and exercise self-discipline, and you will be successful as a freelance broadcaster.

b. LOOKING TO THE FUTURE

Rapid advances in broadcast and sound recording technology can be expected during the next couple of decades. The consumer market, as long as it remains the motivating force behind these improvements, will offer ever better and cheaper machines that will make your work easier. As a professional radio journalist, you will be able to use this super technology to full advantage. The only problem with improving technology, though, is that it costs money to keep updating your equipment. There's nothing you can do about that. The fees you receive will keep you in state-of-the art tape recorders and other equipment.

The future looks bright, technologically speaking. It also looks bright as far as new and continuing work opportunities are concerned. People are hungry for facts, opinions, and entertainment. Information is a growth industry. There's always room for one more broadcast journalist.

APPENDIX

SAMPLE PROPOSAL

February 14, 198-   [ADDRESS
                                                 AND DATE]
Jurgen Hesse
66 Any Street
Vancouver, British Columbia
Canada V3V 1X2

ROYALTY!   [TITLE]

A CBC Radio Special Projects proposal by
Jurgen Hesse, submitted to Bill Terry through
Don Mowatt in Vancouver.   [RECIPIENT]

ROYALTY! will be an aural feast, a glorious   [PRECIS]
celebration of blue blood. We want to find out
everything about ROYALTY! in power and
in absentia: how they rule; what money means
to them; are they really different from us; do
they serve a purpose; are they decent folk; why
do they appear to crave luxury; do they
deserve their fate at the blade of the guillotine
or at the whim of the revolutionary council;
should we admire them; are they real vis-a-vis
the peasant?

Your obedient servant aims to visit and spend
time with such ROYALTY! as Gerald Gros-
venor, 6th Duke of Westminster; the Marquis
Dino Frescobaldi, near Florence; Johannes
Baptiste de Jesus Maria Miguel Friedrich
Bonifazius Lamoral, 11th Prince of Thurn
und Taxis at Schloss Sankt Emmeran,

127

Regensburg, Germany; Jean Louis, Marquis de Ganay, master of Courances, France; Franz Josef, Prince of Liechtenstein, and Their Serene Highnesses Crown Prince Hans-Adam and Princess Marie of Liechtenstein, in Vaduz; and Victoria Eugenia, Duchess of Medinaceli, fourteen times a Marquise, sixteen times a countess, four times a Viscountess, and eleven times a Grandee of Spain, and Luis, Duke of Santisteban del Puerto, heir to the Dukedom of Medinaceli.

[INTERVIEWEES]

May I point out, modestly, that I speak also German, French, Italian and some Spanish.

[QUALIFICATIONS]

ROYALTY! is meant to be a sound feast with the ambient sounds and the music found on the premises. If we can find out the answers to these questions, we will ask, what do these people think of themselves, of the world, of their bloodline, of their future, of their hereditary rights, of their detractors, of their castles and art treasures, of their roles in history, of the loss of their power, of working for a living. But we also want to hear them talk and play, entertain and argue.

[TOPIC DESCRIPTION]

We want to fashion an extravaganza whose aural persona is unmistakably aristocratic — the voices in ROYALTY! will have that undefinable timbre of people in command of themselves and of their environment, and they will find an echo in the host, a person who can match that patina. Richard Burton, were he alive, would be such a host. John Gielgud, Glenda Jackson, Maggie Smith, Jeremy Irons — someone with a British accent, since ROYALTY! is located in the UK and Europe.

[TRAVEL]

We are limited as to the kind of components we can use: voices, music, sounds; but there the limitation ends. ROYALTY! will progress like a centipede — some parts to appear to rest

128

while others rush forward. My idea is to have the components dictated by their own pace. Some will be hectic and driving, others laid back; here speed, there slow pace; and the whole of the parts will move briskly; a tense confrontation here ("But what really happened to Anastasia?"); a William Hamilton, MP, barbed comment there. Always, around it, just as in *Amadeus*, music and sound and ambiance of the environment. Pieces of musicals, operettas, operas as long as they are concerned with ROYALTY! Throughout, as well, there will be surprises, things made to happen that are not expected, irreverent escapades into the realm of fiction or fancy.

What ROYALTY! hopes to be is a footloose document, but not at a footloose price. The project fee is standard as scheduled and open to negotiation.   [FEE]

The feature could be completed for the Fall season, specifically, for September 15, 198-.   [COMPLETION DATE]

_____   [SIGNATURE]

SAMPLE SCRIPT (Partial)

ANNOUNCER And now, "Special Occasion" presents "The Last Run of the Orient Express — Train of Kings, King of Trains," prepared by Jurgen Hesse in Vancouver.

SOUND *Begins:*

NARRATOR (*Over*) This is the story of a journey on a train — the Direct Orient Express. The journey begins in Paris at 11:53 p.m. — seven minutes to midnight.

(*Pause*) We will arrive in Lausanne early tomorrow morning, later in the afternoon Milan, then Venice, Zagreb, Belgrade, Sofia and finally Istanbul — probably six or seven hours late — in three days.

(*Pause*) It is more than a journey through space, it is a journey through time. The train began in 1889, was included as part of the Versailles Treaty in 1918 and carried kings, princes, duchesses, spies and smugglers. The train we are on tonight bears little resemblance to the luxury trains of even forty years ago. There is no dining car, only one sleeping coach. There are no barons aboard tonight, no spies, none of the characters from Graham Greene, Ian Fleming or Agatha Christie. We are leaving Paris nearly one month to the day before the last train — a writer, a photographer, a sound engineer and a producer.

SOUND *Continues*

TAPE *Begins: Bulgarian language. . .*
runs: 1.52
Ends: Orient Express

TAPE *Begins:* The Orient Express is. . .
runs: 1.29
Ends: . . . trains run by Mr. Pullman

TAPE	*Begins:* When I was a child. . . runs: 1.24 *Ends:* . . . it was a great event
TAPE	*Begins:* Après guerre, i y avait. . . runs: .50 *Ends:* . . . to have found freedom
TAPE	*Begins:* The first trip the. . . runs: 1.37 *Ends:* . . . carry a gun in their luggage
TAPE	*Begins:* We are running a special. . . runs: 1.11 *Ends:* . . . stewards and cooks
TAPE	*Begins:* In 1889 the railway. . . runs: 1.14 *Ends:* . . . till Warsaw and Prague
TAPE	*Begins:* With no food or water. . . runs: 2.45 *Ends:* . . . wiedersehn, ciao, dovidjenia
TAPE	*Begins:* La durée du voyage. . . runs: 1.58 *Ends:* . . . done that all his life

*   *   *

NARRATOR	Milan is our first major stop and right away the harsh reality of train travel intrudes after a partial night's sleep and an improvised sandwich breakfast. The conductor distributes handbills written in Italian, French, German and English: "Italian State Railways. Notice: Also within the railways we have to register an increase in thefts. Things are often stolen by taking advantage of crowds during the getting in and out of trains or during the running of trains when passengers are inattentive. Pay attention therefore to your valuables and luggage and help us to prevent thefts by informing at once the railway officials or police about eventual irregularities or suspicious circumstances."

131

SOUND	*Train prepares to stop*
TAPE	*Begins:* It was crazy, we were. . . runs: .50 *Ends:* . . . in it, and their travellers' cheques

*   *   *

NARRATOR	Not long before our next stop in Venice, Nikolas, the Yugoslav couchette conductor arrives in near tears and tells us in German that an elderly passenger in the compartment next to ours is missing his retarded son. Somewhere between Verona and Padua the father had fallen asleep. When he woke up, the son, all the money, and both passports had disappeared. Frantically, Nikolas and the old man searched the entire Orient Express, without success. Now, as we approach Venice, the father will get off, notify the police and start the search.
SOUND	*Train stopping*

*   *   *

SOUND	*Train starts*
ANNOUNCER	The Orient Express pulls out of Venice station at 16.52 p.m. Next stop: Trieste at the border of Yugoslavia.
TAPE	*Begins:* We hopped on the train. . . runs: 2.37 *Ends:* . . . were very thankful about
TAPE	*Begins:* In 1950, one morning of. . . runs: 1.40 *Ends:* . . . so this is a real story
TAPE	*Begins:* Are you aware that. . . runs: 1.30 *Ends:* . . . offer you payment? No

ANNOUNCER   Every time the Orient Express pulls into Villa
             Opicina at the frontier, it stops for an hour or
             two, or three. The Yugoslav border guards have
             started their search for contraband, for smuggled
             blue jeans and transistor radios. Prices are
             cheaper by half in Italy, and every day hundreds
             of Yugoslavs board the train to cross the frontier
             for the bargains.

                         *   *   *

ATTENTION   *End of first reel*

ANNOUNCER   The Orient Express leaves Belgrade at 11.37 in
             the morning two hours late. The train is packed
             with people and baggage of every sort.

NARRATOR   "Yugoslavians are so dirty," one of our Bulgar-
             ian fellow travellers remarks as he throws an
             empty beer bottle out the window. "It will be a
             pleasure to be in Sofia once again." We all laugh
             and hide our Bulgarian money.

                         *   *   *

NARRATOR   Charles Fairbanks wrote more than a hundred
             years ago that "foreign travel ought to soften
             prejudices and liberalize man's mind; but how
             many there are who seem to have travelled for
             the purpose of getting up their rancour against
             all that is opposed to their notions. . ." As we
             pulled into the outskirts of Istanbul, the legend-
             ary city seemed to us a monumental disappoint-
             ment. Was this the centre of the great Ottoman
             empire that reached from the gates of Vienna to
             the Persian gulf? The overwhelming environ-
             ment of poverty reached beyond our outer layers
             of sophistication. Unlike the poor of Yugoslavia
             and Bulgaria who seemed always at work or
             play, these poor were waiting. Waiting for what?

             (*Pause*) As we arrive in the station, we see a large
             banner: "Welcome Orient Express." The banner

seems new. Later we find out it's meant for another Orient Express, the luxury version operated by a Swiss entrepreneur Albert Glatt.

ANNOUNCER Albert Glatt sits in the Istanbul Hilton with a tweed hat in one hand and a cool drink in the other saying: "I dislike capitalists but I like their money. . ."

TAPE *Begins:* We will start this train. . .
runs: 4.08
Ends: . . . he came back for his souvenir

TAPE *Begins:* This is one of the major. . .
runs: 3.05
Ends: . . . price for what you want, you know

TAPE *Begins:* We were standing in the. . .
runs: 1.19
Ends: . . . times a day call to prayer

TAPE *Begins:* We're in Taksim Square. . .
runs: .46
Ends: . . . quite a lot of violence

NARRATOR While Jurgen talks to Gerry Golland about the military presence, I see a sniper on the roof opposite our hotel. Our cameras are upstairs. In the time it takes to run up and unpack a bag, run back down and focus the lens, I would miss the two men I see now — in one frame — a Moslem kneeling and bending to the call of the Muezzin only ten feet from the position of the sniper —Hear no evil, see no evil — it applies to us as well, who have been forbidden by the army to record outside the station. Oh, Gautier, where were you when you described Istanbul as "the most beautiful skyline that undulates between Heaven and Earth," Or, where were we?

SOUND *Tanks increase then fade*

ANNOUNCER May 1 riot in Taksim Square, Istanbul: 38 dead — 200 wounded — 400 arrested.

TAPE	*Begins:* The Direct Orient Express. . . runs: .40 *Ends:* . . . Bulgarian couchette car
TAPE	*Begins: Bulgarian language.* . . runs: .50 *Ends:* . . . felt very much by all the people
ANNOUNCER	The Direct Orient Express from Paris to Istanbul has ended its last run, but the legend is very much alive in the books and memories of those who worked and travelled on it. Trains from Belgrade will continue to arrive in Istanbul, but the through coaches, the famous Wagons-Lits, will be gone forever. (*Pause*) For their most generous assistance we wish to thank Sally Turner, Jean des Cars, Paul Bianchini and Dagmar Kaffauke, the Italian State Railways, Radio Zagreb, Radio Belgrade, the Bulgarian State Radio Commission, and many conductors, passengers and engineers along the way. "The Last Run of the Orient Express" was conceived and prepared for "Special Occasion" by Jurgen Hesse, written and produced by Don Mowatt with the technical assistance of Lars Eastholm and Gerry Stanley in the Vancouver studios of the CBC. My name is Judy Piercey.
NARRATOR	And my name is Christian Bernard.

*   *   *

SELF-COUNSEL SERIES▶

01/87

NATIONAL TITLES:

_____ A Nanny For Your Child	
_____ Abbreviations & Acronyms	5.95
_____ Aids to Independence	11.95
_____ Asking Questions	7.95
_____ Assertiveness for Managers	8.95
_____ Basic Accounting	5.95
_____ Be a Better Manager	8.95
_____ Best Ways to Make Money	5.95
_____ Better Book for Getting Hired	9.95
_____ Between the Sexes	8.95
_____ Business Guide to Effective Speaking	6.95
_____ Business Guide to Telephone Systems	7.95
_____ Business Writing Workbook	9.95
_____ Buying (and Selling) a Small Business	6.95
_____ Civil Rights	8.95
_____ Collection Techniques for the Small Business	4.95
_____ Complete Guide to Being Your Own Home Contractor	19.95
_____ Conquering Compulsive Eating	5.95
_____ Credit, Debt, and Bankruptcy	7.95
_____ Criminal Procedure in Canada	14.95
_____ Design Your Own Logo	9.95
_____ Drinking and Driving	4.50
_____ Editing Your Newsletter	14.95
_____ Entrepreneur's Self-Assessment Guide	9.95
_____ Family Ties That Bind	7.95
_____ Federal Incorporation and Business Guide	14.95
_____ Financial Control for the Small Business	6.95
_____ Financial Freedom on $5 a Day	7.95
_____ For Sale By Owner	4.95
_____ Forming/Managing a Non-Profit Organization in Canada	12.95
_____ Franchising in Canada	6.50
_____ Fundraising	5.50
_____ Getting Elected	8.95
_____ Getting Sales	14.95
_____ Getting Started	11.95
_____ How to Advertise	7.95
_____ How You Too Can Make a Million . . . In the Mail Order Business	8.95
_____ Immigrating to Canada	14.95
_____ Immigrating to the U.S.A.	14.95
_____ Importing	
_____ Insuring Business Risks	3.50
_____ Keyboarding for Kids	7.95
_____ Landlording in Canada	12.95
_____ Learn to Type Fast	9.95
_____ Managing Your Office Records and Files	14.95
_____ Managing Stress	7.95
_____ Marketing Your Service	
_____ Media Law Handbook	6.50
_____ Medical Law Handbook	6.95
_____ Mike Grenby's Tax Tips	6.95
_____ Mortgages & Foreclosure	6.95
_____ Musician's Handbook	7.95
_____ Parents' Guide to Day Care	5.95
_____ Patent Your Own Invention	21.95
_____ Photography & The Law	7.95
_____ Practical Guide to Financial Management	6.95
_____ Radio Documentary	
_____ Ready-to-Use Business Forms	9.95
_____ Resort Condos	4.50
_____ Retirement Guide for Canadians	9.95
_____ Small Business Guide to Employee Selection	6.95
_____ Start and Run a Profitable Beauty Salon	14.95
_____ Start and Run a Profitable Consulting Business	12.95
_____ Start and Run a Profitable Craft Business	10.95
_____ Start and Run a Profitable Home Typing Business	9.95
_____ Start and Run a Profitable Restaurant	10.95
_____ Start and Run a Profitable Retail Business	11.95
_____ Start and Run a Profitable Video Store	10.95
_____ Starting a Successful Business in Canada	12.95
_____ Step-Parent Adoptions	
_____ Taking Care	7.95
_____ Tax Law Handbook	12.95
_____ Tax Shelters ·	6.95
_____ Trusts and Trust Companies	3.95
_____ Upper Left-Hand Corner	10.95
_____ Using the Access to Information Act	5.95
_____ Word Processing	8.95
_____ Working Couples	5.50
_____ Write Right!	(Cloth) 5.95 / (Paper) 5.50

PROVINCIAL TITLES:

Please indicate which provincial edition is required.

Divorce Guide
☐B.C. 9.95 ☐Alta. 9.95 ☐Ont. 12.95 ☐Manitoba ☐Saskatchewan

Employee/Employer Rights
☐B.C. 6.95 ☐Alberta 6.95 ☐Ontario 6.95

Fight That Ticket
☐B.C. 5.95

Incorporation Guide
☐B.C. 14.95 ☐Alberta 14.95 ☐Ontario 14.95 ☐Man./Sask. 12.95

Landlord/Tenant Rights
☐B.C. 7.95 ☐Alberta 6.95 ☐Ontario 7.95

Marriage & Family Law
☐B.C. 7.95 ☐Alberta ☐Ontario

Probate Guide
☐B.C. 12.95 ☐Alberta 9.95 ☐Ontario 11.95

Real Estate Guide
☐B.C. 7.95 ☐Alberta 7.95 ☐Ontario 7.95

Small Claims Court Guide
☐B.C. 7.95 ☐Alta. 7.50 ☐Ont. 7.50

Wills
☐B.C. 6.50 ☐Alberta 5.95 ☐Ontario 5.95

Wills/Probate Procedure
☐Man./Sask. 5.95

PACKAGED FORMS:

Divorce
☐B.C. 9.95 ☐Alta. 10.95 ☐Ont. 14.95 ☐Man. ☐Sask.

Incorporation
☐B.C. 12.95 ☐Alta. 14.95 ☐Ont. 14.95

☐Man. 14.95 ☐Sask. 14.95 ☐Federal 7.95

☐Minute Books 17.95

Probate
☐B.C. Administration 14.95 ☐B.C. Probate 14.95 ☐Alberta 14.95 ☐Ontario 15.50

☐Rental Form Kit (B.C., Alberta, Ontario, Sask.)   5.95

☐Have You Made Your Will?   5.95

☐If You Love Me Put It In Writing   Contract Kit   14.95

☐If You Leave Me Put It In Writing   B.C. Separation Agreement Kit   14.95

☐Sell Your Own Home (Alberta)   4.95

NOTE: All prices subject to change without notice.

Books are available in book and department stores, or use the order form below.

Please enclose cheque or money order (plus sales tax where applicable) or give us your MasterCard or Visa Number (please include validation and expiry date.)

(PLEASE PRINT)

Name _____

Address _____

City _____ Province _____ Postal Code _____

☐Visa / ☐MasterCard Number _____

Validation Date _____ Expiry Date _____

If order is under $20.00, add $1.00 for postage and handling.

Please send orders to:

INTERNATIONAL SELF-COUNSEL PRESS LTD.   ☐Check here for free catalogue.
1481 Charlotte Road
North Vancouver, British Columbia
V7J 1H1

AMERICAN
ORDER FORM
SELF-COUNSEL SERIES

10/86

NATIONAL TITLES

____ Abbreviations & Acronyms	$ 5.95
____ Aids to Independence	11.95
____ Asking Questions	7.95
____ Assertiveness for Managers	8.95
____ Basic Accounting for the Small Business	5.95
____ Be a Better Manager	8.95
____ Between the Sexes	8.95
____ Business Guide to Effective Speaking	6.95
____ Business Guide to Telephone Systems	7.95
____ Business Writing Workbook	9.95
____ Buying (and Selling) a Small Business	6.95
____ Collection Techniques for the Small Business	4.95
____ Conquering Compulsive Eating	5.95
____ Design Your Own Logo	9.95
____ Entrepreneur's Self-Assessment Guide	9.95
____ Exporting from the U.S.A.	12.95
____ Family Ties That Bind	7.95
____ Financial Control for the Small Business	5.50
____ Financial Freedom on $5 a Day	7.95
____ Franchising in the U.S.	5.95
____ Fundraising for Non-Profit Groups	5.50
____ Getting Sales	14.95
____ How You Too Can Make a Million in the Mail Order Business	8.95
____ Immigrating to Canada	14.95
____ Immigrating to the U.S.A.	14.95
____ Keyboarding for Kids	7.95
____ Learn to Type Fast	9.95
____ Managing Stress	7.95
____ Musician's Handbook	7.95
____ Parent's Guide to Day Care	5 .95
____ Photography and the Law	7.95
____ Practical Guide to Financial Management	6.95
____ Ready-to-Use Business Forms	9.95
____ Resort Condos & Time Sharing	4.50
____ Retirement in the Pacific Northwest	4.95
____ Start and Run a Profitable Beauty Salon	14.95
____ Start and Run a Profitable Consulting Business	12.95
____ Start and Run a Profitable Craft Business	10.95
____ Start and Run a Profitable Home Typing Business	9.95
____ Start and Run a Profitable Restaurant	10.95
____ Start and Run a Profitable Retail Store	11.95
____ Start and Run a Profitable Video Store	10.95
____ Starting a Successful Business on West Coast	12.95
____ Taking Care	7.95
____ Upper Left-Hand Corner	10.95
____ Word Processing	8.95
____ Working Couples	5.50

STATE TITLES

Please indicate which state edition is required.

____ Divorce Guide
    ☐ Washington (with forms) 12.95 ☐ Oregon 11.95

____ Employee/Employer Rights
    ☐ Washington 5.50

_____ Incorporation and Business Guide
    ☐ Washington 11.95 ☐ Oregon 11.95
_____ Landlord/Tenant Rights
    ☐ Washington 6.95 ☐ Oregon 6.95
_____ Marriage and Family Law
    ☐ Washington 4.50 ☐ Oregon 4.95
_____ Probate Guide
    ☐ Washington 9.95
_____ Real Estate Buying/Selling Guide
    ☐ Washington 5.95 ☐ Oregon 3.95
_____ Small Claims Court Guide
    ☐ Washington 4.50
_____ W...
    ☐ Washington 5.50 ☐ Oregon 5.95

PACKAGED FORMS

_____ Divorce
    ☐ Oregon Set A (Petitioner) 12.95
    ☐ Oregon Set B (Co-Petitioners) 12.95
_____ If You Love Me — Put It In Writing 7.95
_____ Incorporation
    ☐ Washington 12.95 ☐ Oregon 12.95
_____ Probate
    ☐ Washington 9.95
_____ Will and Estate Planning Kit 5.95
_____ Rental Form Kit 3.95

All prices subject to change without notice.

☐ **Check here for free catalog**

(PLEASE PRINT)

NAME _____

ADDRESS _____

CITY _____

STATE _____

ZIP CODE _____

Check or Money Order enclosed. ☐

If order is under $20, add $1.50 for postage and handling

Please send orders to:

SELF-COUNSEL PRESS INC.
1303 N. Northgate Way
Seattle, Washington, 98133